GATHERING
THE
PIECES

ALSO BY ERNEST DAVE BENNERMAN

Get Fired UP!

He Said, She Said

Stop the Insanity

Brain Booster

GATHERING

THE

PIECES

Relentless Faith to Overcome
Life's Challenges

Ernest Dave Bennerman

Ignite Publishing
New Port Richey, FL 34652

**Gathering the Pieces: Relentless Faith to Overcome Life's Challenges /
Ernest Dave Bennerman. -- 1st ed.**

Library of Congress Control Number: 2017948817
ISBN-10: 0-9976639-3-6
ISBN-13: 978-0-9976639-3-8

Dedication

I would like to dedicate *Gathering the Pieces* to the thousands of people who have allowed me to share the Good News, and to the millions who will be saved and set **FREE** by hearing the Good News of Jesus Christ!

To the King of kings and the Lord of lords, my Lord, Jesus Christ—may Your Kingdom and Your will be done on earth as it is in heaven.

Contents

Introduction

"The world will not be destroyed by those who do evil, but by those who watch them without doing anything." ~Albert Einstein

God is good all the time! Thank you all for making this book part of your library. You have so many books to choose from, yet we're so glad you made this wise choice.

In this book, I will share 17 plus years of ministry. There's no secret, I want people to wake up to the fact that Satan wants their souls. He wants to destroy your families, he wants to afflict you with sickness, and then blame God for it. God had given Adam, and Eve, ruler ship over the garden of Eden. However, Adam and Eve forfeited their right to rule Earth because of SIN. The last Adam, Jesus Christ, manifested in the flesh as a Man, walked in all power and authority so that mankind can rule earth once again. The King wants His sons and daughters to dominate the earth with God's nature and influence. That is where you and I come in; as believers, we are commissioned to advance God's nature and combat the forces of darkness. The devil is an unemployed Angel, who became so full of himself he selfishly led a rebellion in heaven and as a result of his disobedience to God was banded from heaven.

The bible says, "The thief cometh not, but for to steal, and kill, and to destroy: I am come that they might have life, and that they might have it more abundantly." (John 10:10 KJV)

I know, growing up as a child, we think Satan wears red pajamas and carries a pitchfork. When in essence the devil actually masquerades as an angel; he puts on a disguise to fool the world.

And no wonder, Satan himself masquerades as an angel of light. (2 Corinthians 11:14 NIV)

No wonder Satan hates the word of God and the people of God, because it exposes him for what he truly is. He is a coward and he wants to deceive mankind, but **LIGHT** exposes the darkness. It's time for us to cultivate Earth with the Glory of God.

But seek ye first the Kingdom of God, and his righteousness; and all these things shall be added unto you. (Matthew 6:33 KJV)

Every believer has the power to change the culture around them by living a victorious life; Jesus is the first fruit of the believers, so we may expand the Kingdom of Heaven—HIS country— here on Earth. It's time to throw off any doubt or unbelief and begin to **soar like an Eagle**. This book is about your hidden potential. We all have been given the responsibility to reach others with the Good News of the Kingdom of God—the governing influence of a King. Jesus made a way for us to be right in the eyes of God. Pick up your head and be all God called you to be, in doing so we can impact our neighborhoods, cities, and the nations with the culture of the Kingdom of Heaven. Our greatest impact can be achieved through prayer.

> *Our Father in Heaven, hallowed be your name, your kingdom come, your will be done, on earth as it is in heaven. Give us today our daily bread. And forgive us our debts, as we have forgiven our debtors. And lead us not into temptation, but de liver us from the evil one. (Matthew 6:9 NIV)*

Satan wants us to be ignorant of his plan by having us fall in love with this world's system, seeking prestige through, fame, fortune, alcohol, drugs, sex, and money with no purpose. It's time to stop *trying* to be right with God and just *be* right with God.

> *Lest Satan should get an advantage of us: for we are not ignorant of his devices. (2 Corinthians 2:11 KJV)*

It's time to put your faith to work. As you read through the pages, remember how important you are to God. I pray you will not close your mind to the words written on these pages. I pray you will be transformed by the renewing of your mind. Jesus came so that our minds and our hearts can be renewed.

> The bible says, "Have a new mind and heart. Be a new person. That new person has been made like God. He does what is right and holy because he knows the truth." (Ephesians 4:23-24 WE)

I want to thank God for all He continues to do in my life and in the lives of others. I've been excited to write this book for some time now. God allowed me to share with the world my encounters with ordinary people and others, dear to my heart, who encountered the supernatural. I will also share how God continues to use others, like me, to evangelize to strangers at the malls, parks, door-to-door, and around the world. You will read real stories of God healing a woman of a cancerous tumor, deliverance for those who were oppressed, depressed, and possessed by evil spirits. Most people probably don't believe in miracles; however, once I share with you what I and others have experienced, things will become clearer to you.

> The bible says in Matthew 18:11 (NKJV), "For the Son of Man has come to save that which was lost."

I will share miracles that have taken place in my life and in the lives of others. I will also share encounters with Angels and Demons. This book is not about demonology but to encourage you to fight the good fight of faith. We're at war with a realm of unseen evil. However, it is just as real as the seen realm. As an Evangelist, minister of the Gospel of Jesus Christ, God has others and me around the world to seek and save that which is lost. The power of God is the one to save. We are being deployed to go out and be the body of Christ. Let your testimony loosen Satan's grip and set free every person bound up by his demonic forces.

> The bible says in Jeremiah 1:5 (NKJV), "before I formed you in the womb I knew you; Before you were born I sanctified you; I ordained you a prophet to the nations."

God called me as an Evangelist. This is the season for the manifestation of the sons of God. Please keep an open mind and realize we're in the last of the last days. Jesus will return soon. We want to reach as many people as we can with the gospel of Jesus Christ. I want you to know, according to the word of God, "All scripture is given by inspiration of God, and is profitable for doctrine, for reproof, for correction, for instruction in righteousness." (2 Timothy 3:16 NKJV)

Look around. We see signs of devastation in the lives of people all around the globe. The Kingdom of God opposes Satan's kingdom of darkness, which is the reason Jesus, as the Son of God, came down to earth to destroy the work of the devil. Adam and Eve dropped the ball and as a result of their sin, Jesus came down, manifested in the flesh of a man, the "Lamb of God". However, when He comes again, He will be back as the "Lion" from the tribe of Judah. He will judge this world in righteousness and truth. No one is righteous, according to God's Holy standards, except Jesus; we have all disobeyed God due to the sin that has been passed down from Adam & Eve from generation to generation.

> The bible says, "As it is written: None is righteous,
> no, not one" (Romans 3:10 NKJV)

The devil played all of us like a drum; we've been bamboozled by believing in his tactics that try to undermine the Power of God in our lives. Now is the time to educate ourselves and share with others the **Truth** of God's word.

> Jesus Christ said to him, I am the way, the truth,
> and the life. No one comes to the Father except
> through me. (John 14:6 NKJV)

Jesus came down to reestablish his Kingdom here on earth as it is in Heaven.

> The bible says, "But seek first the kingdom of
> God, and his righteousness; and all these things
> shall be added to you. (Matthew 6:33 KJV)

Enjoy this book, everyone. God Bless you all! The goal of this book is to transform the lives of each reader. I pray these principles are applied in the lives of each person. We have a world, lost without the knowledge of the truth, found only through Jesus Christ alone. I challenge every person to break out of your comfort zone and explore this wonderful, but dangerous, life of an *On Fire Believer*. You will get ridiculed for sharing your faith. Do not get bent out of shape if people twist your words. Do not retreat to or climb back into your shell. Let me show you a few examples, different approaches I've used to develop dialog with strangers. Don't worry about trying to be perfect. You will make some mistakes; nevertheless, you will find yourself being more effective in getting your message across as you go along. Never allow discouragement to take root when sharing your faith. Don't be afraid to display your imperfections so the person you are ministering to will give you some slack. You must realize the walls are coming down; you don't seem so much of a threat to those you minister to. If you seem like a "know-it-all", they will say anything to get you off their back. Beware, somebody's life will be at stake as God utilizes you to be a vessel to this lost world.

Please NOTE: The names in this book have been changed to protect the identity of the individuals.

Poker Face

"I alone cannot change the world, but I can cast a stone across the
waters to create many ripples." ~Mother Teresa

I have worked many years as a job coach. This particular day, I was conducting training with several
young people. This older man, in his mid-seventies,
walked toward me with a limp and a huge scar down the
right side of his face. Mr. Jim (not his real name) would
sing spiritual songs every week, while coaching five
young people at this facility. After two weeks of training, I got irritated every time I heard this old-timer sing.
He prompted me, so I asked him this question. Look,
Mr. Jim I asked, Why are you so cheerful? He said, "I'm
glad you asked, young man. Many years ago, I used to be
a heavy drinker; I loved to gamble, living life on my
terms."

Mr. Jim expressed to me, many years ago, he invited his best friend and his girlfriend for a night of poker. Mr. Jim's buddy started complaining about losing money during the card game. He stated that his friend accused him of cheating, so one thing led to another, and they started fighting. His friend picked up a chair and slammed it down on Mr. Jim's head. He kicked him in the ribs; Mr. Jim was hurt badly, lying in his own blood. His friend reached into his pocket and took all the cash he'd won in the card game. His friend wore a pair of boots and used the heel of his boot to assault him viciously. He lost his left eye. He crawled on the carpet, trying to get away, afraid he might die. Fear gripped his heart as his life flashed before his eyes. He kept repeating again that his friend maliciously crushed his eye. It became obvious that Mr. Jim's friend was dealing with some personal battles he failed to conquer.

Mr. Jim told me he was in and out of consciousness, while he was lying in his own pool of blood. The young lady who was there with my friend urgently ran out and called 911.

The paramedics arrived.

They tried to stop the bleeding.

They immediately performed CPR; as the ambulance rushed Mr. Jim to a nearby hospital.

He shared something with me about the supernatural that was hard for me to believe at first. I was clueless about the afterlife; however, Mr. Jim said he died in the hallway, while waiting to be treated. He said his spirit left his body; he stared down at his dead corpse, and he immediately heard the doctors talking about how they tried many times to get his heart to respond. He also told me his senses were clear, and the colors he saw in Heaven were remarkable. He said he was standing next to an Angel; he cried out to God to give him another chance. Suddenly, the Angel led him back into his body. He woke up and noticed a linen sheet covering his face. He yelled out to the orderly, who was attending to other patients.

Mr. Jim shared this incredible story with me while eating lunch. I could not believe how much he remembered about his out of body experience. He recalls observing the doctors discussing his life. He was in bad shape. At this point, he had lost a lot of blood, and the hope of saving his life was very slim. He said, while he was out of his body, he saw his heart stop beating many times throughout this ordeal. Mr. Jim has a new lease in life, because of the power of God.

> Jesus said, I have told you these things, so that in me you may have peace. In this world you will have trouble. But take heart! I have overcome the world. (John 16:33 NIV)

Mr. Jim shared his story with tears running down his cheek. I have seen nothing like it before. His skull was crushed badly, but he survived this ordeal.

No body but God could have performed this miracle.

What an amazing story!

He has every reason to be thankful. Look how God used this man, bringing him through all of this trauma, and allowed Mr. Jim to share his testimony with me. Mr. Jim could have given up on life, but he refused to allow his disfigurement to be a crutch. He's truly a blessing in my life. A few months later, after he shared his story with me, I gave my life to God. Hallelujah! ☺

> *Wherefore comfort yourselves together, and edify one another, even as also ye do. (1 Thessalonians 5:11 KJV)*

I Want to Go Home

One Sunday morning, a very fragile church Mother (aka CM) sat down next me; I asked her why her leg was swelling up. She felt compelled to tell me that she died and came back to life during her stay at the hospital.

Dave: What do you mean you died and came back to life?

CM: I became ill, and they rushed me to the hospital.

Dave: What happened?

CM: The hospital gave me a series of tests and things went badly. I died and my spirit left my body. I saw myself lying there in the bed, the next moment, I saw the gates of Heaven. The city looked so beautiful. No human words can describe the beauty or brilliance. I told the Angel standing next to me, "I'm ready to go home." The angel said, you cannot go inside. Your time to go is not now. You will go someday, but not right now. I felt very sad because I did not want to go back to earth. The angel said, God still had much work for me to do, then I can join them.

Amazing witness of the power of God, this 86 years old lady did not play; her eyes had a sparkle that no individual can dim. Wherever she goes, she shares her story with whoever will listen. I thank God; He placed wonderful people in my life to share all that God wants to do for his children.

Heaven is a real place, and I long to see this place, but we have the power to live a full and victorious life now, on Earth. We must be about our Father's business. We need to reach the world for Jesus Christ and represent the Kingdom of God. When I share my faith with those I have encountered, I try to make sure I do everything in my power to share the Ten Commandments (God's moral law) in love (heartfelt) not pride. They're going to die if I do not inform them they are carrying a deadly disease called SIN. Jesus is the cure.

Let me share what Jesus has done for sinners in hope that conviction of sin will bring true salvation.

But, before I go any further I want to pause for a second because many people have responded with, "I look awesome." But I go deeper than physical appearance. First, I always make sure I speak to people in a compassionate way because my intentions are not to drive you or anyone else away, but to share with you the Good News of Jesus Christ.

Let's resume, remember how crushed you were by your own iniquity. Many souls are prisoners in this evil world full of depravity in a cesspool of sin. Humility is the key when anyone addresses "SIN" with people they may encounter at the supermarket, bank, doctor's office, school, or on their job. God replaces our sin with his purity, if you are a child of God; HE no longer sees your sin.

> God's way is perfect. All the Lord's promises prove true. He is a shield for all who look to him for protection. (2 Samuel 22:31 NLT)

The Unseen World

I heard a very wise person say, you can lead a horse to water, but you can't make him drink, unless you give him plenty of oats to eat. You have to continue to be a beacon of light to this world, so people will be drawn to God. One thing about a thirsty person, if they are thirsty enough, they will be ready to drink.

What bothers me is that according to Dr. Bill Bright of Campus Crusades for Christ, only 2 percent of Christians share their faith on a regular basis; we have to change that right now. Each born-again believer has a moral responsibility to warn each lost soul we come in contact with that hell is real. The bible says to tell the truth in love. If I love you I have to share the Good News about Jesus Christ and the Kingdom of God. There are gospel tracts floating around about how God is good and he has a great plan for your life, without addressing our sin nature.

My wife and I were searching for a house few years ago before we bought the home we live in now. We looked on the MLS listing and saw this beautiful house that had all the bells and whistles. We drove to the house and noticed the house to be exactly as advertised, except for the location of the house being in the middle of a drug infested neighborhood. You might look good on the outside, but just like the house I've talked about, you can't allow any trace of sin in or around your life.

> *For I was born a sinner—yes, from the moment*
> *my mother conceived me. (Psalms 51:5 NLT)*

God loves us so much He will not let us bring SIN into the Kingdom of Heaven. Many saints of the Christian faith have gospel tracts and messages preaching only about his love. I'll be the first to say "Amen", but God must point out our sin nature to us. We hear 90% grace and 10% addressing sin. The correct way might be to touch on the Ten Commandments (God's Moral Law) in love, 90% on addressing sin and 10% grace. If we do that, this person will clearly understand how much God really loves them. Jesus died for us and took our place by giving us a new life, so we can go tell others about His wonderful love. When I heard the real gospel of Jesus Christ, I didn't need to look back on my old life and stay there. There's a story in the bible about Lot's wife fleeing from the wrath to come, warned by the Angel not to look back because of the "SIN" of this wicked city. "The Lord rained upon Sodom and upon Gomorrah with brimstone and fire from the Lord out of heaven, and he overthrew those cities, and all the plain, and all the inhabitants of the cities, and that which grew upon the ground." (Gen. 19:24-25)

*But his wife looked back from behind him, and
she became a pillar of salt. (Gen 19:26 KJV)*

You must be dead to your old life to enjoy this new life
in Jesus Christ. We must show the love of Christ by tell-
ing the truth. We all disobeyed God, and we need a Savior. We need to know this, so we can take sin seriously.
Each person we share our faith with needs to know that
sin has terrible consequences. Passion is the key if we
want to impact this world for the Kingdom of God. We
have to take responsibility for the treasure that lies on
the inside us for change to take place in our community.
Stop saying you are not ready; God will give you the
grace to succeed when you step out in faith and share
what you truly believe. Time is running out on us all. We
must reach this world for the glory of God.

*Lord reminds me how brief my time on earth will
be. Remind me that my days are numbered—how
fleeting my life is. (Psalms 39:4 NLT)*

Let me ask you a question. Are you willing to be committed to working with God in saving a soul and bringing transformation? You have seeds of greatness that
need to be planted in the heart of a human soul. Take a
leap of faith. You have to learn to love the unlovable, and
when you take the initial step, God will take another
step to make sure His agenda is accomplished. I want
you to think big, but start small, by asking them their

name. One way to break the ice is by addressing natural things; move in next by asking this question...

If you die today, do you know if you're going to Heaven?

Most people are so afraid of what people think of them, they do nothing. This book is here to challenge you to step out in faith and know you are part of what God wants to do in the lives of people. If you are not working for God, then you are working for the enemy.

The scripture says, "For the sinful nature is always hostile to God, for it does not submit to God's law; indeed, it cannot." (Romans 8:7 NLT)

You have endless ability to

create new actions.

CHAPTER 2

Phone Line

"God has placed you where He has placed no one else. No one else in the world has the same relationships you have. No one will stand in the same grocery store line at exactly the same moment you do. No one else will come across a hungering diplomat in the desert at exactly the same time you do. God hasn't put you in those places merely to model the truth. Listen for the voice of the Spirit to whisper in your ear. Watch for the stranger on the road. And be aware of your opportunities to go where He would send you."
~Chuck Swindoll

I jumped into my car before heading to work, volunteering at a local call center for prayer. This particular morning differed from any other morning. I stopped for a cup of coffee, and as I pulled into the parking lot, I felt God as I entered the call center. We had a group of awesome prayer warriors, believing God to move in a powerful way for this ministry. People from all over the world would reach out for intercessors to come into faith agreement for whatever need they believed God for.

The next call would have a major impact on me for the rest of my life. I picked up the phone, and the person on the other end was a lady, named Shirley. I could hear from her shaky voice that she was in tears.

I asked her, "What would you like God to do for you?"

Shirley: I went to the doctor and he said I have breast cancer. They detect a huge mass on my right breast, but I know God is a Healer.

Dave: Shirley, lay your hands on your breast, where they spotted the mass. We curse cancer in the name of Jesus. Shirley, right now, God is healing you.

The phone went quiet for 10 seconds. She began to cry out loud with joy.

Dave: Shirley, tell me what's going on.

Shirley: I feel heat.

Dave: What do you mean, you feel heat?

Shirley: I feel heat flowing through my body.

Dave: anything else?

Shirley: The lump is getting smaller, Oh my God! It's Gone!

She's weeping with joy.

Shirley: What's your name?

Dave: Dave

Shirley: I will let everyone know you were available to receive my call for prayer this morning.

Dave: Glad to be of service. King Jesus gets all the glory.

If you are sick, we curse sickness; right now, be healed in Jesus' name.

> He was pierced for our transgressions, he was crushed for our iniquities; the punishment that brought us peace was on him, and by his wounds we are healed. (Isaiah 53:5 NIV)

Time to awake from our slumber, and take our place as children of light. This fallen world is full of sin and wickedness, due to the fall in the Garden of Eden. Adam and Eve sinned because they believed Satan's lie, thinking there was something more enjoyable to life than what Almighty God was giving them. If you are a believer, take your rightful place and take authority over evil spirits and principalities.

Death and life are in the power of the tongue, and those who love it will eat its fruit. (Proverbs 18:21 NKJV)

You might be facing a situation like Shirley, right now; trust God to work things out to fulfill His purpose in the earth. Maybe, you have lost a loved one to cancer or to a deadly disease, and you believed God would heal them, but they died. I want to say, I am sorry for your loss. I have lost loved ones and friends to sickness and disease as well. My answer to you is, I DON'T KNOW why some get healed and others don't. I can say God knows everything, and nothing catches Him off-guard regarding your life. Keep believing and keep trusting in God to do mighty things in your life for His name's sake.

Father, if you are willing, please take this cup of suffering away from me. Yet I want your will to be done, not mine. (Luke 22:42 NLT)

My heart is confident in you, O God; my heart is confident. (Psalm 57:7 NLT)

The Lord is close to the brokenhearted and saves those who are crushed in spirit. (Psalms 34:18 NIV)

He heals the brokenhearted and bind up their wounds. (Psalms 147:3 NIV)

Do not let your heart be troubled. You believe in God; believe also in me. (John 14:1 NIV)

Demon Showed Up in Church

Let me share with you something I witnessed in one of my meetings during service. We had many people who would come up for prayer, several hundred people. This young woman walked up to the Man of God. She manifested this evil spirit and started cursing at this preacher. I'll never forget the look on this preacher's face. The hair on his arm must have stood up.

For God hath not given us the spirit of fear, but of power, and of love, and of a sound mind. (2 Tim 1:7 KJV)

This preacher took a second to comprehend what was happening, and he shouted:

"Devil I command you to come out, right now, in the name of Jesus."

The man of God, repeated to this demon to come out of this woman as she used every curse word in the dictionary. The demon kept yelling louder and louder, until finally, the evil spirit left her. Praise God!

Behold, I give unto you power to tread on serpents and scorpions, and over all the power of the ene-

my, and nothing shall by any means hurt you. (Luke 10:19 KJV)

If you are a born-again believer, you have power and authority to do what this man of God has done in Jesus' name. You must live a holy, righteous life and stay away from the works of the flesh.

> *Now the works of the flesh are manifest, which are these; Adultery, fornication, uncleanness, lasciviousness, idolatry, witchcraft, hatred, variance, emulations, wrath, strife, seditions, heresies, envying, murders, drunkenness, revellings, and such like: of the which I tell you before, as I have also told you in time past, that they which do such things shall not inherit the kingdom of God. (Galatians 5:19-21 KJV)*

If you're going to do amazing things for God, do not allow distractions to fill your mind with anything other than God's voice.

> *For the Lord is a great God, and a great King above all gods. (Psalms 95:3 KJV)*

He wants to use us as able vessels to bring His work to pass. I will say again, keep the communication lines open, because you never know who will be on the other line. Satan's job is to keep you so busy with what's going around you that the very thing you have been hoping for might be right in front of you.

When you have direct contact to God, don't allow anything or anyone to stop your flow and stop allowing the devil to harass you. When you are married, you don't want anything or anyone coming between you and your spouse. I want to ask you a question. What's distracting you from hearing God? Don't get so busy that you fail to hear the warning bells going off in your spirit. We have to become mission-minded, always expanding the Kingdom of God.

> *Anyone with ears to hear should listen and understand! (Matt 11:15 NLT)*

Hidden

Here's a different approach to witnessing to those men and women in the telemarketing industry, for example. Many times throughout the week, telemarketers would call me, and I would quickly hang up the phone. I know sometimes you may come across an individual who can become very annoying, and you might be tempted to slam the phone in their ear. If you are ready to keep the phone lines open, I challenge you to minister the Good News of the Kingdom to these people; they're just like you and me. Telemarketers are excellent people to share your faith with and not feel afraid if you're doing things the wrong way. Think about it this way; if things go downhill, ask if you can pray that he or she would have an incredible week in sales. Who's going to turn that down? Moreover, you still sowed seeds into their life. They're trained to offer a service and not be moved by rejection if someone rudely hangs up the phone.

Today is a good time to practice sharing the gospel. We must think outside of the box. Lives are uncertain; we must reach people by any means necessary. God want us to convey His image and likeness on the earth. I say to myself often, *"Lord, you sure you have the right one?"* God is looking for a yielded vessel to this lost and broken world to display this same Kingdom from heaven. I'm challenging each person to step out of their comfort zone and reach this dying world, so they will not go to hell. We have to be broken for the soul of every person who crosses our path; you don't have to be a big shot preacher to be used by God. He will use whoever is available to be an Agent of Change. Let's dive into some training.

Telemarketer: Hi, my name is Sally; we have a fabulous offer for you and your family. Am I talking to Mr. Bennerman?

Dave: Yes.

Telemarketer: We have a wonderful special for you.

Dave: Wow! I want to hear more, but before you start, can I ask you a question?

Don't panic. Usually, they will allow you to ask questions, because they desire the sale.

Telemarketer: Sure.

Dave: If you die tonight, do you know if you would go to heaven?

Telemarketer: Yes.

Dave: Fantastic, how do you know that?

Telemarketer: I'm a good person. I go to church, Sir; I need to go over our product, services, or special offer.

Don't panic. Their calls are being monitored; they have to stick with the script.

Dave: My apologies, I want to hear more about your product or services or special offer. Do you consider yourself a good person?

Telemarketer: I go to church, Mr. Bennerman. I need to show you more about this offer.

Religious people talk like this; you must have a personal relationship with Jesus Christ. It is possible this person had a false conversion.

Dave: Thank you for your patience. I'm ready to hear more. Can I give you a good person test?

Telemarketer: Phone disconnected.

"They will never accept grace till they tremble before a just and holy law." ~Charles H. Spurgeon

I want to share with you a story in the bible regarding a woman named Rahab. She was a Harlot! We're going to keep it real. This promiscuous woman was held captive in that lifestyle. She lived within the outer city walls of a wicked city; they practiced wickedness that displeased God. The children of Israel were **told** by God to **occupy** the land that **God promised to give them** after 40 years in the wilderness after the Israelites spent 400 years in **slavery.**

*God is no respecter of person; he can show mercy to anybody.

> Then Joshua secretly sent out two spies from the Israelite camp at Acacia Grove. He instructed them, "Scout out the land on the other side of the Jordan River, especially around Jericho." So the two men set out and came to the house of a prostitute named Rahab and stayed there that night. (Joshua 2:1 NLT)

Business was booming, all night, 24 hours a day. She was labeled a rebel, the black sheep of the family. Most of her money was made during the night. But God used Rahab to hide the spies in her home.

> But someone told the king of Jericho, "Some Israelites have come here tonight to spy out the land." So the king of Jericho sent orders to Rahab; bring out the men who have come into your house, for they come here to spy out the whole land.
>
> Rahab had hidden the two men, but she replied, "Yes, the men were here earlier, but I didn't know where they were from. They left the town at dusk, as the gates were about to close. I don't know where they went. If you hurry, you can probably catch up with them." (Actually, she had taken them up to the rooftop and hid them beneath bundles of flax she had laid out.) So the king's men went looking for the spies along the shallow crossings of the Jordan River. And as soon as the king's men had left, the gate of Jericho was shut. (Joshua 2:2-7 NLT)

*Rahab decided to walk away from her trashy lifestyle and run into the arms of an awesome God.

*No need to beg sinners to come to Jesus. Once they see how sinful they are, they will cry out for his mercy and grace.

Before the spies went to sleep that night, Rahab went up on the roof to talk with them. "I know the Lord has given you this land, she told them. We are all afraid of you. Everyone in the land is living in terror. For we have heard how the Lord made a dry path for you through the Red Sea, when you left Egypt. And we know what you did to Sihon and Og, the Amorite kings east of the Jordan River, whose people you destroyed.

No wonder our hearts have melted in fear! No one has the courage to fight after hearing such things. For the Lord your God is supreme God of the heavens above and the earth below." (Joshua 2:8-11 NLT)

Rahab acknowledged the God of the Israelites is the one true God.

Rahab was willing to lose her life by lying to the authorities.

Rahab was willing to lay down her life to gain eternal life.

Rahab was willing to turn from her old life and take on a new life.

"Now swear by the Lord you will be kind to me and my family, since I have helped you. Give me

some GUARANTEE when Jericho is conquered, you will let me live, along with my father and mother, my brothers and sisters, and all their families."

> *"We offer our own lives as a guarantee for your safety," the men agreed. "If you don't betray us, we will keep our promise and be kind to you when the Lord give us the land." (Joshua 2:12-14 NLT)*

*See, when we make a commitment, it always cost us something. Jesus offered up his life that we may have life.

> *When we come into the land, you must leave this scarlet rope hanging from the window through which you let us down. And all your family members—your father, mother, brothers, and all your relatives—must be here inside the house. (Joshua 2:18 NLT)*

*The red rope was a type and shadow of the blood of Jesus.

Rahab extended her kindness to the spies by finding the very rope she *might have* used to perform evil acts (sex parties), now is the very thing to be the sign of safety for her and her entire household. God can turn your trashy life and make pure treasure. Praise God! The very thing I use for evil, I now use for good. You were created to do better, add value to those you come into contact with. You don't want to live your life any other way. You are part of the family of God with a purpose for your life.

"If they go into the street and are killed, it will not be our fault. But if anyone lays a hand on people inside this house, we will accept the responsibility for their death. If you betray us, however, we are not bound by this oath in any way." (Joshua 2:19-20 NLT) Stay in the house; stop doing drugs, stop opening the door to evil spirits to wreck your life. Keep all doors and windows shut, because if you do not follow instructions, what happens to you will be your own doing.

> *You, who love the Lord, hate evil! He protects the lives of his godly people and rescues them from the power of the wicked. (Psalms 97:10 NLT)*

> *"I accept your terms," she replied. And she sent them on their way, leaving the scarlet rope hanging from the window. (Joshua 2:21 NLT)*

*The blood of Jesus is able to redeem "Whomsoever." I don't care what you might be into, what type of lifestyle you had in the past.

God can take a prostitute and make her a prominent child of the King.

Rahab was her own woman.

Rahab believes the Israelites serve the one true living God.

Rahab was willing to walk away from the pain of regret and birth a life of promise.

Rahab, made a choice to pursue righteousness, when the opportunity showed up at her front door.

The opportunities do not discriminate. You have to be ready to answer the call when opportunities show up in your life. You must take a step of faith.

Like Rahab, embrace opportunities for you and others to be a blessing to the world they live in. There is no shortcut when it comes to taking a stand on your faith.

Rahab risked her life for the greater good because she believed better is on the way.

Faith without works is dead. (James 2:14 NKJV)

Difficult moments will test your character. You have to step out of your comfort zone and focus on the mission of Jesus Christ, who left us to complete it, and then the end will come. Make today count; share the love of Jesus Christ. Invade the work place with this philosophy, and soon, we'll suffocate the evil that's trying to bombard us.

Rahab did things that most folks will shake their heads at, but realize, you might be worse than Rahab. Don't be slothful when opportunity comes knocking on your door. You have to be ready to make a move. Show me what you are working with. Anybody can behave good when they have no problems but what happens when a crisis comes, challenging what you believe. Don't let your brain stop you from sharing the gospel of Jesus Christ. Don't let self-doubt rob you of your potential to perform at a high level. Not in your own ability, but in His ability.

But without faith it is impossible to please him: (Hebrews 11:6 KJV)

Rahab decided to break away from bad behavior and obtain new behaviors. She heard all the rumors about the victories the Israelites were eager to manifest. They had nothing to lose other than what God cannot use. Is there something in your life that's hindering you from being all that God called you to be? God wants to know if you will trust him with your life, be the hands, feet, the body for his glory. By The Law, human nature is sinful. God was going to kill everybody in the city, but when grace and truth showed up, Mercy saved Rahab and her family.

Don't waste time worrying about needless things.

CHAPTER 3

Hateful Face

"Darkness cannot drive out darkness only light can do that. Hate cannot drive out hate only love can do that."
~Martin Luther King, Jr.

While going out into the mission field around the inner city, I met a teenage boy around 16 years old with the word "HATE" written on his forehead and a bag of money tattooed on the side of his face. One of the keys to effective evangelism, for me, is to have an exchange. These are great ice breakers. When you're witnessing, you have to ask questions, build a rapport with the person you're engaging. You have seconds for them to know that you are not a nut case. Here's how the conversation went.

Dave: Hello, young man.

Mark: What's up!

Dave: We're in the neighborhood giving away food. Do you know anyone who's interested in a bag of food?

Mark: Not interested.

Right now, I'm looking at his body language to see if I need to go further into the conversation.

Dave: Do you go to school?

Mark: Not anymore.

Dave: The reason I ask you this question is because I see you have a heart for art.

Don't judge his tattoo; I'm encouraging him. You must allow room for God to work.

You must find a common ground to keep the conversation going. Make sure you're polite with a gentle smile. Have good eye contact. If you have sunglasses on, please remove them, so they can see your eyes.

Mark: What do you mean?

Dave: I noticed your art work. Must have taken a long time, Huh?

Mark: Yeah, my boy, Malik, did the work. *See how the walls are coming down?*

Dave: You have a good eye for art regarding your tattoo. *warm smile

Mark: I like being different.

Dave: Hey Mark, can I ask you a question? *Don't proceed without permission; this approach separates you from being religious or judgmental. Remember, we have the Holy Spirit; allow Him to move.

Mark: Sure!

*Yes!! Now I'm ready to plant some seed. Remember, God saves; we're just an instrument to be used while the Great Physician is working.

Dave: When you die, do you know if you are going to Heaven?

Mark: I don't know.

Dave: Would you like to know?

Mark: Yes!

Dave: Hey Mark, do you consider yourself a good person?

Mark: Yes! I used to do bad things, but I try to do my best to be good.

Dave: Can I ask you three questions to see if you are a good person?

Mark: Sure!

Dave: How often have you told a lie?

Mark: 50 times.

Dave: What do you call a person who tells lies?

Mark: Liar.

Dave: Have you stolen anything, no matter how small it is?

Mark: Too many to count.

Dave: What do you call a person who steals?

Mark: A thief.

You notice that I'm not accusing Mark of anything. He's voluntarily answering the questions. God has given him a conscience.

I share this illustration to show you have to engage people when sharing your faith. The reason I've taken him to the law is to destroy any self-righteousness, pride he may carry.

> *For whosoever shall keep the whole law, and yet offend in one point, he is guilty of all. (James 2:10 KJV)*

The law is like a mirror to show us how wicked we are before God. You may be a good person, according to other people's standards, but they do not set the bar; God does. The bible says you have to be more righteous than the Pharisees (Religious leaders).

> *For I say to you, that unless your righteousness exceeds the righteousness of the scribes and Pharisees, you will by no means enter the kingdom of heaven. (Matthew 5:20 NKJV)*

> *For God so loved the world that he gave his only begotten Son, that whoever believeth in him should not perish, but have everlasting life. (John 3:16 KJV)*

The gospel message is the power God uses to save us. If we're going to reach this lost world, we cannot be ashamed of the gospel. He died for those who knew about him and for those who did not.

> *For I am not ashamed of this Good News about Christ. It is the power of God at work, saving everyone who believes—the Jew first and also the Gentile. (Romans 1:16 NLT)*

I want to stop there for a moment and make sure you pray to God about what to say or not to say. Be excited about yielding your talents and services unto the Lord. Amen!

> *And he said to them, Go ye into the entire world and preach the gospel to every creature. (Mark 16:15 KJV)*

Tattoo Evangelism

You never know who may cross your path. It's amazing when I look at sinful people hating one another. The young man I ran across earlier in this chapter tattooed his face full of hateful words. He might have been an abused child, maybe his peers called him a loser. Or, he might have been rejected many times. He expressed himself through art. I can relate to this young man in many ways. I was called a loser and was the butt of people's jokes. I became very self-conscious of who I am. I got a tattoo because I wanted to fit in and make my place in life.

*Be careful not to let the world define who you are.

Think for a moment. What if God allowed you to go through all the trouble regarding your health, finances, relationships, rejection, and foolishness to save you and heal your broken heart for such a time as this? God sends you back well-equipped to invade the environment with the Kingdom of God. Be patient with people and realize you were a mess when he pulled you out from under the bridge. He wants to raise leaders to represent His nature and likeness.

Let's check out what the bible says regarding tattoos:

> *You shall not make any cuttings in your flesh for the dead, nor tattoo any marks on you: I am the Lord. (Leviticus 19:28 ESV)*

In no way am I condemning anyone. I want to let you know that was not God's design for your life; however, now that you know the truth, if you have a tattoo, use it as a witnessing tool to lead someone to God. You may have dealt with a painful past; maybe you were sexually abused when you were a little girl or boy. God can use your painful past to set you and others free from shame, guilt, low self-esteem, and physical abuse.

The enemy wants you to stay in the closet and die within, but I'm here to tell you Jesus has set you free. You have only to say, "Jesus, here I am in all my brokenness. You died so I may have life and have it more abundantly. Today, no running. I completely surrendered to you. I repent of my past and trust in the only one to save me and set me free. I received this new life as a gift, which you died for me two thousand something years ago in Jesus name." You can now walk in this new life and connect to a bible believing, bible teaching church that will encourage you and lead you to a place of maturity in the body of Christ.

Make sure you are sold-out to this life as an Ambassador for Jesus Christ. You need to know you will have setbacks, you will have disappointments, and most people will think you are weird, but that's okay.

You must catch hold of the vision God has for humanity.

*Vision will enable you to keep daily focus on seeking the lost to be saved.

*Vision will enable you to be faithful putting God's agenda first.

*Vision will enable you to focus your eyes on Jesus.

*Without commitment, you will never start being a soul winner for Christ JESUS.

If you want to be effective for the Kingdom of God, you must allow setbacks to build your character, so you can be well-prepared for the mental battles you will face as you allow the Holy Spirit to live through you. We are here to take back what the enemy has stolen from us. Give your best to whatever God has given you and be laser-focused on saving lives from the kingdom of darkness.

For the Lord is coming to judge the earth. He will judge the world with justice and the nations with fairness. (Psalms 98:9 NLT)

During times of stress opens the windows for times of growth, so take the first step by being obedient to God. He wants the whole world to see his glory.

CHAPTER 4

Lady in the Window

"When Jesus saw their faith, he said, friend, your sins are forgiven." ~Luke 5:20 (NIV)

One rainy day in Florida, my wife and I were conducting a bible study; we had a great time teaching God's word to the local community. As we were wrapping up, this shadowy figure appeared looking through the window with glossy eyes. We walked over to her and asked, what is your name? She kept pacing back and forth and grinding her teeth. She walked away, so I looked at my wife, she looked at me, and we realized this lady was possessed by a demon. We were packing up our notes from bible study and guess what? She appeared standing near the door. I have to admit she was very creepy, so we were very cautious how we approached her.

This lady yelled, "I hate you both. God is not real."

She cried out to us, "I tried to kill myself last night several times by jumping out in front of traffic."

This demonic spirit tried to kill her, but God wanted to save her soul.

I quickly remembered the story about the little boy who was demon possessed.

In this bible story, "One of the men in the crowd spoke up and said, Teacher, I brought my son so you could heal him. He is possessed by an evil spirit that won't let him talk. And whenever this spirit seizes him, it throws him violently to the ground. Then he foams at the mouth and grinds his teeth and becomes rigid. So, I asked your disciples to cast out the evil spirit, but they couldn't do it."

"Jesus said to them, you faithless people! How long must I be with you? Bring the boy to me. How long has this been happening? Jesus asked the boy's father. He replied, Since he was a little boy. THE SPIRIT OFTEN THROWS HIM INTO THE FIRE OR INTO THE WATER, TRYING TO KILL HIM. Have mercy on us and help us, if you can." (Reference scriptures Mark 9:17-22 NLT)

I spoke to this evil spirit tormenting this woman. I said, "You will not have her; right now, in Jesus' name, come out of her and be made whole."

Her eyes rolled back, which made the hair on my arm stand up. I laid my hands on her head, and that evil spirit left in Jesus' name. The foul demon shouted with a loud cry, and a minute later, she was in her right mind with tears of joy. We prayed the prayer of faith regarding salvation, and she surrendered her life to Jesus Christ. Praise God! We must be ready at all times. You never know if you have to cast out a demon in Jesus' name.

> *And these signs will accompany those who believe: In my name they will drive out demons; they will speak in new tongues. (Mark 16:17 NIV)*

Let me share something with you. People from all walks of life are hurting. The time for playing around with the things of God must stop. There are people like this woman, jumping off bridges, taking drugs, alcohol, sex, and greed, clueless about why God created them.

Be Ready

You must have a clear understanding that God wants to use you 24 hours a day, seven days a week. Somebody might say, "Hey, God said I can rest on the Sabbath."

Yes! You should recharge your battery and get your proper rest, but realize we should be ready at all times to represent God's work.

> *But Jesus answered them," My Father is always working, and so am I. (John 5:17 NLT)*

Let me use a good example in my own life of what Jesus is talking about. My wife and I traveled on a cruise to Mexico for our anniversary to enjoy ourselves; however, we both had to allow God to govern our lives, the decision regarding our activities. We needed to be compassionate to the person who was cleaning our rooms and the cooks who were preparing our food. That's what Jesus was talking about when he said, The Father is always working and He's working as well. I remember the story about how the religious leaders tried to accuse Jesus of working on the Sabbath (Day of Rest).

> *One Sabbath day as Jesus was teaching in a synagogue, he saw a woman who had been crippled by an evil spirit. She had been bent over for eighteen years and was unable to stand up straight. When Jesus saw her, he called her over and said," Dear woman, you are healed of your sickness! Then he touched her, and instantly she could stand straight. How she praised God! But the Lord replied, You hypocrites! Each of you works on the Sabbath day! Don't you untie your*

ox or your donkey from its stall on the Sabbath and lead it out for water? This dear woman, a daughter of Abraham, has been held in bondage by Satan for eighteen years. Isn't it right that she be released, even on the Sabbath? (Luke 13:10-16 NLT)

It's very important that you let the word of God talk to you. Jesus is the one doing the talking. No matter where you go, look for opportunities during your downtime to do good and not evil. Be bold for Jesus Christ; keep that momentum going, so we can impact this generation and generations to follow. I want you to be courageous. Things do not happen overnight, but if you will have that never die attitude, with the help of the Holy Spirit, you will have the boldness to chase every devil out of every neighborhood, out of every major city.

The Time is NOW!

It's time for Kingdom citizens to take back our inheritance, which is occupied by the enemy. When we do that, our cities will be safe; our schools will be safe. We have to be aggressive in our approach by being productive Kingdom people on our jobs, communities, schools, and churches. We need to implement Kingdom ideas and Kingdom logic into the market place.

Stop thinking too much and start doing, because lives are uncertain. Change must start with us. You are a brand-new Lamborghini in the garage, ready to burn rubber, because it was created for adventure. The life of a believer is adventurous in every way. I want you to be sold-out for God and allow Him to use you for His Kingdom agenda.

The world sees Citizens of God as chumps.

HE sees us as Champions!

Don't be moved by what you see; don't fear the impossible. It's just a long word, so no more excuses. You have all of heaven backing you to take back our streets, take back our schools for the Kingdom of God.

> *The Lord gives his people strength. The Lord blesses them with peace. (Psalm 29:11 NLT)*

Make peace with your past so it won't disturb your present.

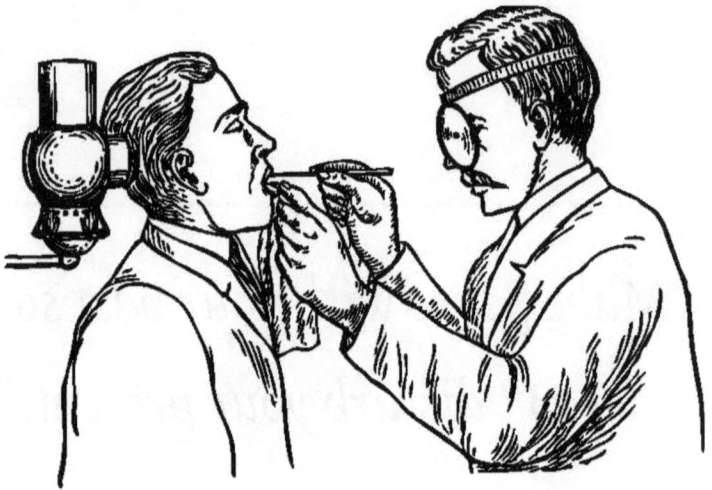

CHAPTER 5

Is There a Doctor in the House?

"Demons run when a good man goes to war." ~Steve Moffat

I was making my rounds, praying for people at a local medical office, when I noticed a tall man, walking into the waiting room, very disoriented. I was conversing with a patient, when this young man walked past me recklessly. The mother looked so exhausted trying to keep up with this young man. I asked her if there's anything I can do. "I consulted several doctors in the mental field and nothing seems to help my son." She quietly said to me, "Several weeks ago, my son would try to jump out of the moving car and grab the steering wheel, hoping to crash. The only way for me to get rest is to load him up on medication. He would behave like a walking zombie." I sat down to talk with this young man. He would pace back and forth at an incredible pace, which made the other patients uncomfortable.

Finally, the doctor called this young man and his mother into his office. Ten minutes later, the doctor asks me to come inside the room. As I walked in, we gazed at each other.

This young man stared at me with the look of pure evil.

I shouted, "COME OUT of this man, devil, IN JESUS' NAME!"

He started hissing at me in a mighty way. He was getting louder and louder.

Every time I brought up JESUS, he would hiss even louder, grinding his teeth. The mother gave me a fearful look, exhausted.

I looked back at her son and said with boldness, "Devil, I said, in JESUS' NAME, let him go, right now."

He let out a loud scream, and suddenly, he was in his right mind. Praise God!

> And the unclean spirits, whenever they saw Him,
> fell down before Him and cried out, saying, "You
> are the Son of God." (Mark 3:11 NKJV)

We must remember, there are two kingdoms existing, the Kingdom of Heaven going up against the kingdom of darkness. Satan is the head the kingdom of darkness; he's behind the system of this world.

> As he (Jesus) spake these words, many believed on him. Then said Jesus to those Jews which believed on him, if ye continue in my word, then are ye my disciples indeed; and ye shall know the truth, and the truth shall make you free. They answered him, we be Abraham's seed, and were never in bondage to any man. (John 8:30-33a KJV)

We have to realize, we belong to another world. God had an original plan with Adam and Eve, but through disobedience, they fell in the garden and sin entered the human race. God had given man authority to rule the animals, things, and resources, but not people. We are made in the image and likeness of God. The last Adam, the Christ Jesus manifested in the flesh, operated in the power and authority to show every born-again believer how to rule the earth. Jesus stripped Satan of his devices, and he snatched the keys from the enemy's hands and gave them to those who are sons and daughters of God.

> You are of God, little children, and have overcome them, because He who is in you is greater than he who is in the world. (1 John 4:4 NKJV)

We need not be fearful of the enemy or his devices. We are here to take over and manifest the Kingdom of God to its rightful place. Jesus did not carry long dialog with evil spirits. He said shut up and come out of him or her.

Look at the living conditions in the inner city...drugs, violence, murders, and rapes. We can look at the upper classes and see homes are falling apart; drugs, pedophilia has increased in the areas where you think families are supposed to feel safe. Evil is rampant, the kingdom of darkness is trying to stake its claim.

No more! The Kingdom of light is here to take back our neighborhoods, communities, our nation, and the world. We have to say what the Word says and be bold for Christ Jesus.

> Death and Life are in the power of the tongue: and they that love it shall eat the fruit thereof. (Proverbs 18:21 KJV)

We are not here to take sides but to take over in Jesus' name. We have a new sheriff in town, and His name is King Jesus the Son of the living God.

Remember, the devil and his demons fear powerful believers, who refuse to let the enemy walk over them. Enough is enough. The devil has been killing from the very beginning, but for us to sit back and take what is being thrown at us, has to stop right here.

You are powerful, not pitiful. You are mighty, not messy. You are a champion, not a chump. You are victorious, not a victim.

Stop seeing yourself as the victim and stop walking with your head down, like you are an orphan. No, you are a King's Kid; start acting like one.

Wise words are like deep waters; wisdom flows from the wise like a bubbling brook. (Proverbs 18:4 NLT)

When I was 10 years old, a bully threatened to assault me physically after school. The clock struck 2pm; my palms were sweaty. I felt sick to my stomach, so I asked if I could go to the nurse's office.

Why torture myself? However scared, I went to the bully and took the first swing out of nowhere and clocked him good. You must overpower this unseen enemy who's tormenting you by giving you bad thoughts. Rebuke him in Jesus' name. Pray! Pray! Pray! And take action by doing exactly what God said to do. You always want to have momentum when you're working for the Kingdom of God. You have enough power to raise the dead, so don't limit God. Let Him do whatever he wants to do.

> *Heal the sick, cleanse the lepers, raise the dead,*
> *cast out devils: freely ye have received, freely give.*
> *(Matthew 10:8 KJV)*

No more excuses. It's time to be about your Father's business.

*You were made to believe
for the impossible.*

Sam is Dead

"The fear of the death follows from the fear of life. A man who lives fully is prepared to die at any time." ~Mark Twain

I'm on cloud nine, a solider for Jesus Christ, one afternoon I decided to volunteer at a soup kitchen. You would be amazed at the number of homeless people in need. The atmosphere changed once this egocentric loudmouth, named "Sam", walked in the door. He would show up for daily showers and meals. Here I am, new to the Christian faith, but hungry for the things of God. One of the kitchen volunteers alluded that Sam likes to fake a heart attack, like Fred Sanford from the 70's sitcom 'SANDFORD & SON'. We expressed our pleasantries, and I shared with him the gospel. The conversation went as follows:

Dave: Hello!

Sam: What's going on, young man?

Dave: Do you think much about Heaven?

*I'm shaking in my boots, afraid I might screw up.

Sam: I'm good.

Dave: God loves you!

*I have no clue what I'm doing; just excited Jesus saved me from hell.

*I shared the gospel of Jesus Christ by giving him a gospel tract, called "This is your life." Now remember, I'm new to the whole Christian faith, hoping he will take the tract.

Dave: Hey Sam, I don't want you to die and go to hell. You need to be certain about your eternal destination.

Sam stuck the gospel tract in his pocket, and as he got near the exit, he faked as if he was having a heart attack and laughed as he walked out the door. Moments later, screams filled the dining room area as Sam collapsed and dropped dead. I immediately ran over to him. I could not believe how pale he turned. Prayer went out toward Sam as the ambulance came to transport him to the hospital. The paramedics stayed for 10 minutes, trying to bring him back to life, which is not a good sign; however, they could not do so. The ambulance drove away without the light flashing.

The reason I share this story is that things happen whether we are prepared or not. We have **86,400 seconds in a day.** It's critical that we don't waste one second thinking why we're not effective witnesses for Jesus Christ. Sam kept speaking death until it finally manifested itself. Words are powerful.

> *The tongue can bring death or life; those who love to talk will reap the consequences. (Proverbs 18:21 NLT)*

> *Be careful what you say out of your mouth. And just as each person is destined to die once and after that comes judgment. (Hebrew 9:27 NLT)*

Although Sam moved on to the next life, either condemned or justified; we pray his family made peace by asking Jesus Christ to forgive them for their sins and grant them eternal life.

> *He that believeth on him is not condemned: but he that believeth not is condemned already, because he hath not believed in the name of the only begotten Son of God. (John 3:18 KJV)*

Death is Real

People die every day. **Over 150,000 people die every day.** Hell is real; demons are real. Their job is to depress, oppress, and possess you. Their mission is to draw you and others away from God. They love for you to walk in disobedience and hate you to walk in obedience. You are working either for the Kingdom of light or for the kingdom of darkness. Remember, the enemy is cunning. You may not even know you are being played like a fiddle until it's too late. He will entice you to get your own rope and talk you into hanging yourself. Let's look at what Judas did when he betrayed Jesus.

> *Early in the morning all the chief priests and elders of the people made their plans how to have Jesus executed.*
>
> *When Judas, who had betrayed him, saw that Jesus was condemned, he was seized with remorse and returned the thirty pieces of silver to the chief priests and elders. "I have sinned," he said, "for I have betrayed innocent blood." "What is that to us?" they replied. "That's your responsibility." So Judas threw the money into the temple and left. Then he went away and hanged himself. (Matthew 27:1 NIV)*

Judas was a thief; he allowed a door to open for the enemy to sneak in and cause havoc in his life.

I grew up in New Jersey; I used to hear some of the older people talk about a fictitious man named "JODY". He's the type of man who fabricates his own rules and has no care in the world. JODY, had no job and will take your woman when you are not looking. If you fail to take care of business, you had better believe JODY will slither into your life and tear apart everyone and anything that was dear to you. You cannot give the enemy a place ultimately to destroy you.

> *Do not let the devil control you. (Ephesians 4:27 WE)*

We must make sure we're not building the devil's house with our own tools. He can do nothing unless we cooperate with him. Stop giving him a place, with your disobedience (**work of the flesh**). We have to take on the mind of Christ if we're going to walk in fullness. The devil will use anything or anyone as puppets to further his agenda.

Say, No More!

Say it one more time, No More!

You and I have things to do and places to go for God's Kingdom purposes. You were made to cause havoc to the kingdom of darkness. This book is not about demons but how to walk in the power and authority of God. We have the power to cast out devils and manifest the Kingdom of God.

For whatsoever is born of God overcometh the world: and this is the victory that overcometh the world, even our faith. (1 John 5:4 KJV)

Stop being afraid and walk in the power that God has provided to every believer. Don't come in an agreement with this world by ways of reasoning. We're living in evil times; we must take God at His word.

Wise words satisfy like a good meal; the right words bring satisfaction. (Proverbs 18:20 NLT)

We're living in the last days. Open your spiritual eyes and see what's going on in the world. The devil and his army of demons want you to walk in the flesh, so he can gain access to your life and ultimately your soul.

For the flesh desires what is contrary to the Spirit, and the Spirit what is contrary to the flesh. They are in conflict with each other, so that you are not to do whatever you want. But if you are led by the Spirit, you are not under the law. (Galatians 5:17-18 NIV)

If you're a child of God, lift your head, stick out your chest, and manifest his image and likeness for the whole world to see. Lay hands on the sick, so they will recover. Cast out devils in Jesus' name.

Demons run from you, not the other way around. Let me ask you something. Have you noticed the enemy has infiltrated the entertainment industry with horror movies, X-rated movies, foul mouth comedy, even nudity on mainstream TV? The enemy honestly believes he can abort God's agenda. He cannot stop it, but he will strive to delay it.

> People ruin their lives by their own foolishness and then are angry at the Lord. (Proverbs 19:3 NLT)

God manifested himself in the flesh two thousand years ago and walked 33 ½ years to show us how to live for God, to be an example of how to talk, walk, and love the way He loves.

I was flipping through the channels one evening and saw a show about prison life. These guys committed a terrible crime, but Jesus Christ still loves them. We must share the Good News about what Jesus did for us and the teaching of the Kingdom of God. If you gave your life to Christ and walk in the power of the Holy Spirit, go assist God in getting others free.

> The Spirit of the Lord is on me, because he has anointed me to proclaim Good News to the poor. He has sent me to proclaim freedom for the prisoners and recovery of site for the blind, to set the oppressed free. (Luke 4:18 NIV)

We are the champions!

We have the victory!

WE WIN!

Say it again; WE WIN! GET UP!

Be about the Father's business. We have no disability; we have the **Ability** to resolutely deal with the problem by loving the unlovable, feeding the poor, and clothing the naked. People must be empowered by the Holy Spirit, so they'll live a victorious life. If you want to change the world and preach the gospel of Jesus Christ, you will be hated for Christ's sake. The enemy wants you to ring the bell of defeat. Jesus took our defeat and defeated death on the cross 2000 years ago and rose from the dead. He is victorious and so are you if you put your faith and trust in the one true God who manifested in three persons, The Father, The Son and the Holy Spirit.

This book is to motivate you to take the leap of faith and go for that lost person who does not know Jesus. This book is to give you some tools to encourage you to be a witness of the gospel. You can do this if you believe God has everything for you to succeed. No more excuses. Take the first step and be a **Fool for Christ**. I can think of worse things people have said about me or worse that I said about myself.

*Let this mind be in you which is also in Christ
Jesus. (Philippians 2:5 KJV)*

We all are confronted by fear, but do it anyway, because somebody's life is uncertain. Be consistent in
sharing your faith to those you will meet in this lifetime.
You must push through the barrier. You were born to
make a difference and make this world a better place.
The blood of Jesus redeemed us from the curse of the
law, so we can live a victorious life. You must work to
your potential and get fired up about being part of the
harvest of souls that will come into the Kingdom by your
lifestyle.

Someone is dying every day; you must be serious about
living life to the fullest. What are you going to do with
the **Dash** between your **Birth Day** and your **Death Day?**
*The Dash in the middle is what makes you special.**

*When people do not accept divine guidance, they
run wild. But whoever obeys the law is joy-
ful. (Proverbs 29:18 NLT)*

Dr. Martin Luther King, Jr. stood up for civil rights
and equality for mankind. He stood up for injustices.
He was serious about his **Dash.**

JESUS CHRIST was serious about **HIS DASH,** what
about you? **Time for you to get in the GAME. Two-
minute warning, and we need a touchdown to win**

the game. Unleash the beast and go make a difference now, not later.

Purpose should benefit life
not destroy life.

CHAPTER 7

What Happened to My Drink?

"Do not get drunk on wine, which leads to debauchery; instead be filled with the spirit." ~Ephesians 5:18 (NIV)

I love going out to reach those living in darkness. Here's a story that happened one Friday night, while witnessing to bystanders. I teamed up with several other soul winners for Jesus. I noticed a short fellow, who was staggering a bit. He walked out of the bar holding a cold beer in his hand. I said to this man:

Dave: Hey, my brother.

Stranger: Hey, man.

Dave: My name is Dave. What's yours?

Stranger: Jimmy.

Dave: Nice to meet you. Jimmy. We're here to give away free food and gifts and show the love of God.

Jimmy: I know God!

Dave: Wonderful, my brother.

Jimmy: I worked hard all week long and decided to get me some beer.

Dave: How long have you been walking with God?

Jimmy: Hey, nobody's perfect!
Very important to know, build rapport and wait for the right opportunity. The Holy Spirit brings conviction.

Jimmy: I go to church when I get time.

Jimmy has experienced religion, not a relationship. I never brought up church.

Jimmy: What church you go to?

Dave: I fellowship with other believers who love Christ Jesus. We gather at ABC Church to encourage and empower each other to impact this world in the name of Jesus.

Remember, Jimmy has observed religion, but he's about to encounter God in a powerful way.

Jimmy: Good talking to you. I'm about to enjoy my beer now and go home.

Dave: Jimmy, can I ask you a question before you go?

Always ask for permission before you proceed.

Jimmy: Sure!
Be bold and ask your question. No Fear!

Jimmy: *curious look

Dave: If you died today, would you go to heaven?

I'm allowing the Holy Spirit to move, and I want Jimmy to hear the voice of this wonderful God. Our Heavenly Father does not force himself on anyone.

I see many people try to frighten a person to make a decision. You must operate in the fruit of the spirit and allow His love to take over. Give the Holy Spirit the time to operate. The bible says in Rev. 3:20, *'Behold, I stand at the door and knock. If anyone hears My voice and opens the door, I will come in to him and dine with him, and he with Me."*

Alright, let's get back to the story.

Dave: If you died tonight, where would you go?

Jimmy: I hope to go to the man upstairs.

THIS IS WHAT MOST RELIGIOUS PEOPLE SAY

Dave: Hey Jimmy, can I pray for your eye?
I noticed Jimmy had a patch over his eye, so I asked him if it's okay to pray for his eye.

Jimmy: Sure!

Dave: I come against the spirit of infirmity. I command healing for Jimmy's eye, right now, in Jesus' name. *(The power of God hit that man.)*

Jimmy: Hey something is happening to me.

Dave: What's going on, Jimmy?

Jimmy: I feel weird. What's happening?

Dave: God is healing you, right now, Jimmy.

Jimmy: Wow! Man, I can see. I guess I don't need this beer anymore.

Jimmy kept rubbing his bad eye. His eye started tearing up.

Dave: Jimmy, would you like to receive Jesus Christ as your Lord and Savior?

Jimmy: Yes! I want Him in my life now.

We prayed with Jimmy, and he sat his cold bottle of beer on the ground and walked away praising God.

The power of God is incredible; do not limit our Creator to what He's able to do. He's looking for an able body to be the arms, hands, legs, mouth, every member to be His body. People are dying all over the world; they need to know about this awesome GOD. If God can take a person like me from darkness into light, he can save anybody. We're in the last days, and God is calling His children to take a stand, walk in love, and have the boldness to do the miraculous.

Let me ask you a question. If you are a child of God, are you ready to take a step of faith and display the Kingdom of God? No one can answer that question but you.

Bible says, "Now faith is the substance of things hoped for, the evidence of things not seen." (Hebrews 11:1 KJV)

Make a decision, be sold out for God, and do not be moved by trickery or flattery.

Learn to develop a thick skin, even when you're popular, and don't believe your own resume. Keep moving forward, regardless of the obstacles you may face on this journey with King of kings and Lord of lords. We are Kingdom citizens, who live in this world, but we are not of this world. The body of Christ is not called to be in seclusion, for the fear of contamination, for we are the light of the world.

Focus on Kingdom advancement; what you focus on you strengthen.

We will forever be known by

the tracks we leave behind us.

CHAPTER 8

The Biker

"I'm not perfect, just forgiven." ~Anonymous

One hot afternoon, while soul winning, I must admit, I was a little intimidated by this dude. He looked like "Hell Angels." I asked this man if he needed food or clothing provided by a local ministry.

*It's always best to try to find something to use as a conversation piece, while assisting and ministering the Good News of the Kingdom of God.

Dave: Did you want a bag of food?

Biker: Yeah!

Dave: Can I ask you a question?

Biker: Oh, what is it?

Dave: If today was your last day, would you know for sure that you will go to heaven when you die?

Wait for the answer. The Holy Spirit is at work, bringing forth conviction.

Biker: I was locked up for a long time, but now, I go to a small church in town.

Dave: Great... Have you made Jesus Christ your Lord and Savior?

Biker: I believe so.

Time to make sure he did not encounter a false conversion.

Remember! <u>Ask for permission.</u>

> If you openly declare that Jesus is Lord and believe in your heart that God raised him from the dead, you will be saved. (Romans 10:9 NLT)

*You do not want to force Jesus on them. They have a choice to accept or deny him. The choice is theirs to make, not yours.

Let's get back to this powerful encounter with my biker friend.

Dave: Do you consider yourself a good person? Now remember, I'm not judging you, but how often have you told a lie?

*I'm walking him through several of the Ten Commandments to break up the stony heart. I normally raise my hands in the air and keep them up as I read some of the Ten Commandments to show him I violated His commandments as well.

Biker: More than I can count.

Dave: What do you call a person who tells a lie?

Biker: Liar.

Dave: Hey, friend, I want you to know that I'm not passing judgment on you in any way. I mess up also before God. *It's very important to show how you violate the Law as well.

Dave: Have you ever stolen anything, no matter how small it may appear?

Biker: Yeah! Everybody messes up.

Dave: You're so right; we all have sinned and fallen short of his glory.

Biker: Silence.

*We want to go from his HEAD (Intellect) to his HEART. Mankind believes they can work out their own salvation.

> *For the person who keeps all the laws except one is as guilty as a person who has broken all of God's laws. (James 2:10)* *I found out using the Ten Commandments is effective.*

Dave: Here is the last one. Have you looked at a woman and lusted after her?

Biker: All the time, but I'm going to church now.

Beware of rabbit trails and stay focused on the message.

Biker: Nobody's perfect.

Dave: Jesus is the only one who fulfilled the Law perfectly, and we have not. See, my friend, you just admitted to being a liar and a thief; you also lusted in your heart. Your **SIN** has cut you off from God. If you die now, you will go to **HELL**.

Biker: ? *(questionable look)*

Dave: Will God find you innocent or guilty on the Day of Judgment?

Biker: Guilty.

Dave: Heaven or Hell?

Biker: I guess Hell.

Dave: Does that concern you?

Biker: Very Much.

Dave: What are you going to do?

Biker: Can you pray for me? I've done a lot of bad things in my life. I spent time in prison.

Dave: Lord Jesus, I pray with my new friend. Touch his heart, right now, to receive your Son as his Lord and Savior.

> *Therefore He is also able to save to the uttermost those who come to God through Him, since He always lives to make intercession for them. (Hebrews 7:25 NKJV)*

I'm allowing the Holy Spirit to move in a mighty way and watch God do some amazing things. We cannot save a soul spiritually, but we can be the hands, mouth, feet, and let them see Jesus Christ in us.

> *The Law was our schoolmaster to bring us to Christ, that we might be justified by faith. (Galatians 3:24 NKJV)*

Who's Your Master?

To be effective in these last days, you have one Lord, who's the King of kings and the Lord of lords, and his name is Jesus Christ. Things and people want to scream for your time, but God "Yahweh" must scream the loudest.

To follow Jesus, you have to take up your cross and follow Him daily.

> *Then he said to the crowd, if any of you wants to be my follower, you must turn from your selfish ways, take up your cross daily, and follow me. (Luke 9:23 NLT)*

I cannot tell you how often, I've played these words in my brain. God transforms wonderful people, people who've been abused, raped of the possibilities to influence this world for the greater good. See, you were made to dominate and rule things, not people. The enemy has kept casualties in blindness, so they will forfeit what God wants to do in their life.

> *The thief does not come except to steal, and to kill, and to destroy. I have come that they may have life, and that they may have it more abundantly. (John 10:10 NKJV)*

I want to inform each person who reads this book, the devil and his demons are not playing with you. We live in a fallen world that has turned its back on God, but for such a time as this, He's raising up Kingdom citizens, who have been given power and authority in Jesus' name to operate in the Kingdom of God.

The Spirit of the Lord God is upon me, Because the Lord has anointed me to preach good tidings to the poor; He has sent me to heal the broken hearted, to proclaim liberty to the captives, and the opening of the prison to those who are bound. (Isaiah 61:1 NKJV)

*Use your real testimony. Everybody has a story. You know what God has saved you from when you were enjoying your foolishness for a season. You have the power of the Holy Spirit living inside of you, so take a leap of faith. Stand on eye witnesses of the gospel writers of Matthew, Mark, Luke, John, and the letters of Apostle Paul in the New Testament.

The gospel message is the power God uses to save us.

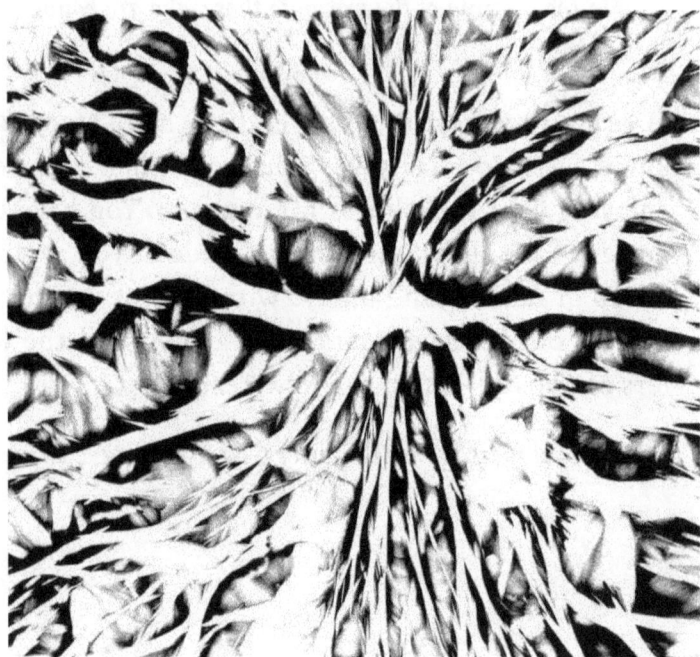

CHAPTER 9

Vision of Hell

"Men's consciences tell them:

There is a dreadful hell, and everlasting pains; where sinners
must with devils dwell, in darkness, fire and chains."
~C. H. Spurgeon

I want to share something that happened to me. To this very day, I get chills. Years ago, around midnight, while lying in my bed, the Lord Jesus showed me in a dream or vision that I needed to warn others of this terrifying place. I was looking at this huge door. As I opened the door, I descended into what looked like some sort of funnel or tunnel. I noticed both sides of the tunnel were filled with smoke so black I could hardly see my hands in front of my face. Suddenly, the fiery flames touched my body, but they did not affect me. Breathing was very difficult as I continued to descend to this dark pit. I looked at the corners, and it appeared to be a dark shadow trying to grab me, but for some reason, the Lord Jesus prevented these evil spirits from grabbing hold of me. I started Praising God like never before. I looked at my hands and arms and noticed the fire could not burn me.

The stench in the place was awful. I heard screams.

These lost souls were crying, "Help me!"

"Help me; get me out of here!"

"Jesus, please give me another chance to turn my life over to God."

I was traveling at such a rapid speed, hearing these screams. God brought me back that night. He allowed me to see these things. I heard one young man, scream at me to save him. I reached out my hand to grab is boney hands. Fire was coming out of his eye sockets; he looked horrible. Several times, I tried to grab him but seemed to come short. Finally, I reached out to him, and God immediately ascended me back up from the pits of hell.

God allowed this man to come back with me, so I laid him on the ground, and he looked like somebody burned alive in a car. He was charcoal black, very hideous. I ran over, got water, and poured it on this young man. I looked, and to my surprise, this man started slowly changing back to his natural self.

Wow! He was a Caucasian man with glasses.

I woke up, wondering what just happened here. My heart was beating like crazy, Lord Jesus; You shared this dream with me to warn others about this place.

> The bible says, *"but others save others with fear, pulling them out of the fire." (Jude 23 NKJV)*

Hell is real, whether you believe it or not. I want you to remember, it doesn't matter what we believe. It matters what is true.

> *There was a certain rich man who was clothed in purple and fine linen and fared sumptuously every day. But there was a certain beggar named Lazarus, full of sores, who was laid at his gate, desiring to be fed with the crumbs which fell from the rich man's table. Moreover, the dogs came and licked his sores. So it was that the beggar died, and was carried by angels to Abraham's bosom. The rich man also died and was buried. And being in torments in Hades, he lifted up his eyes and saw Abraham afar off and Lazarus in his bosom.*

Then he cried and said, Father Abraham, have mercy on me, and send Lazarus that he may dip the tip of his finger in the water and cool my tongue; for I am tormented in this flame; But Abraham said, Son, remember that in your life time you received your good things, and likewise Lazarus evil things; but now he is comforted and you are tormented. And besides all this, between us and you there is a great gulf fixed, so that those who want to pass from here to you cannot, nor can those from there pass to us.

*Then he said, I beg you therefore, father, that you would send him to my father's house, for I have five brothers, that he may testify to them, lest they also come to this place of torment. Abraham said to him, They have Moses and the prophets; let them hear them. And he said, No, father Abraham; but if one goes to them from the dead, they will 'REPENT" (change direction/mindset). But he said to him, if they do not hear Moses and the prophets, neither **will they be persuaded though one rise from the dead.** (Luke 16:19-31 NKJV)*

I am writing this book to warn those to stay away from this awful place and draw closer to God. The worst thing about **HELL** is God will not be there, total separation from the Creator. Those who chose to come to this place will die with all their talents and abilities and never use them to bring God glory. One of the biggest lies Satan tells those who are lost is they have plenty of time to give their life to Jesus Christ, or there are other ways to get to Heaven. My heart breaks when I see the enemy deceiving a lost soul.

> *He who has the Son has the life: he who does not have the Son of God does not have the life. These things have I written to you who believe in the name of the Son of God, so that you may know that you have eternal life. (John 5:12-13a NKJV)*

Jesus became **SIN** for us, so we need not go to this awful place. **Hell** is a real place, separated from God. Now is the time to seek God while He may be found.

> *It is appointed unto men once to die, but after this the judgment. (Hebrews 9:27 KJV)*

Are you trying to tell me you're going to live any way and there are no consequences? Young people don't believe the lie you can party with your friends in hell. The devil is trying to trick you into believing hell is one big party or false preachers who say hell does not exist. I suggest you read your bible and allow the Holy Spirit to speak to your heart. God showed me this horrendous place to warn as many people as possible.

> *The scripture says, WHOEVER was not found written in the BOOK OF LIFE was cast into the LAKE OF FIRE. (Revelations 20:15 KJV)*

Whatever you have to do, do not waste your life on silly stuff that means nothing. Run to Jesus, so you may be forgiven of your sins. The evidence is found in the written Word of God, based on Historical evidence that Jesus walked this earth, died on the cross, and rose from the dead. Your life should be the proof that God is who He said He is.

----

*A good sign of maturity is
when you can take a mess and
turn it into a message.*

Fight for the Glory

*"It doesn't take a hero to order men into battle. It takes a hero
to be one of those men who goes into battle."*
~Norman Schwarzkopf

Many years ago, before God called me to preach
the gospel of Jesus Christ; I received a powerful dream from the Lord. I was living in PA
when I had this dream. I was walking in the inner city,
filled with drugs, alcohol, prostitution, crime, and
shootings. The citizens who lived in the community
were terrorized by rebellious gang members.

This dream seemed so real.

Six young boys approached me. One young man walked
up to me and said...

Gang member: Hey, man, what are you doing here?

Dave: Look, I'm not looking for trouble.

Gang Member: Is that a bible in your hand?

Dave: Yeah!

Gang Member: *(Laughing)* Look what we got here, fellows!

I wanted to get out of there, fearful for my life.

Gang member: What you going to do now, Jesus freak?

All of the sudden, boldness rose inside of me. The fear quickly dissipated. I stared back at this young man.

Dave: I will not deny Jesus Christ as my Lord and Savior.

Gang Member: What!

Dave: I WILL NOT DENY JESUS CHRIST AS MY LORD and SAVIOR!

Ex. Gang member: Hey man, WE ARE FOLLOWERS OF JESUS CHRIST AS WELL!

Dave: Wow!

Ex. Gang member: I gave my life to God once my homeboy got shot dead. I was angry with God and church people. They look at me like they never done anything wrong. I hate these phony people! But God healed my heart; I will serve Jesus Christ for the rest of my life.

Dave: I thought you guys were going to jump me.

Ex. Gang member: Sorry we had to be so hard. We wanted to make sure you were the REAL THING.

God showed me He's stirring up His people to take back what has been stolen from them. God is working on the hearts of these young boys who were former gang bangers; now with a repented heart they're radical for the things of God. If you are part of the body of Christ, don't judge these young people just because they do not look like what you expect. God has raised them up to influence their culture.

> *Man looks at the outer appearance but God looks at the heart. (reference scripture 1 Samuel 16:7 NIV)*

The enemy always fights you the hardest when he knows God has something great.

God is moving in a powerful way, building up men and women, boys and girls to showcase His glory. Do not just believe your time is coming; believe your time is NOW. Every time we share our faith, it's a win/win situation. The only time we lose is when we do not share our faith. The ex-gang bangers had been conditioned to think a certain way due to the evil culture they grew up in. Digest God's environment and watch things change for the good.

Time out for being average; we were created for so much more.

Time out for just doing enough.

Time out for just being enough.

Time out for just producing enough.

God is doing a mighty shaking in this world. The ex-gang members, decided to live their lives for God, even if it results in death.

> Be faithful unto death, and I will give you a crown of life. (Rev. 2:10 KJV)

Here's a story of a young man who wander in unbelief, but watch how God revealed himself to this person, who tried walking with his crutches. I approached him and said...

Dave: Hello, my brother.

Stranger: Hi!

Dave: What happened to your leg?

Stranger: I was playing football and injured my leg.

Dave: Do you believe God can heal?

Stranger: Sure!

I laid my hands on his leg and believed the prayer of faith.

Stranger: *curious Look*

Dave: I speak to every joint, muscle, and ligament in Jesus' name, be made whole.

Stranger: I feel heat.

Dave: What do you mean?

Stranger: The pain is going away.

Dave: Praise God!

Stranger: Thank you!

Dave: Can I ask you a question?

Stranger: Sure!

Dave: Do you think much about the afterlife?

Stranger: Somewhat.

Dave: Do you think you're good enough to go to Heaven when you die?

Stranger: Yes!

Dave: Awesome! Is it because you are a good person?

Stranger: Yes!

Dave: You seem like a good person to me. Can I give you a good person test by asking you three quick questions?

Stranger: Sure.

Dave: If you can put a number on it, how often have you told a lie?

Stranger: A few times.

Dave: What do you call a person that tells lies?

Stranger: Liar.

God has written the laws on their hearts. God has given them a conscious of what is right and wrong.

Dave: Have you stolen anything, no matter how small it was?

(Candy bar, downloads, illegal music etc.)

Stranger: Yes!

Dave: What do you call a person who steals?

Stranger: A thief.

Dave: Have you had lustful thoughts toward a female in your mind?

Stranger: Yes.

Dave: The bible says, if you lust in your heart, you committed adultery in your heart. Have you done that?

Stranger: Nobody's perfect.

Dave: I totally agree with you. The bible says, "No one is perfect, not even one."(Romans 3:10)

Stranger: Who can be saved?

Dave: Every person who put his faith and trust in Jesus as their Lord and Savior. First, you have to do two things:

(1) Repent (Turn away from your sin and turn toward God)

(2) Put your faith and trust in Jesus Christ alone to save you.

Dave: If you want to receive this wonderful Savior who died that you may have life and have it more abundantly, you have to confess that you sinned against God, breaking His holy laws, and desperately need a Savior. Jesus Christ was the only person in the world that never sinned. He became my righteousness. Trade your righteousness for Jesus Christ's Righteousness.

> God so loved the world that he gave his one and only Son, that whoever believes in him shall not perish but have eternal life. (John 3:16 NIV)

Stranger: I need Him.

*He wanted me to pray with him regarding salvation.

*Be sincere and loving when you ask questions. I love this approach to the gospel; always remember the approach Jesus had when He encountered the woman at the well. (John 4)

Let's look at this amazing woman's story about her encounter with Jesus Christ at the well. (John Chapter 4)

Let's pick up in verse John 4:4 (NIV)

> "Now he had to go through Samaria. So he came to a town in Samaria called Sychar, near the plot of ground Jacob had given to his son Joseph. Jacob's well was there, and Jesus, tired as he was from the journey, sat down by the well. It was about noon. When a Samaritan woman came to draw water, Jesus said to her, "Will you give me a drink? (His disciples had gone into the town to buy food.) The Samaritan woman said to him, "You are a Jew and I am a Samaritan woman. How can you ask me for a drink?" (For Jews do not associate with Samaritans.) Jesus answered her, "If you knew the gift of God and who it is that asks you for a drink, you would have asked him and he would have given you living water." Sir," the woman said, "you have nothing to draw with and the well is deep. Where can you get this living water? Are you greater than our father Jacob, who gave us the well

and drank from it himself, as did also his sons
and his livestock?"

Jesus answered, "Everyone who drinks this water will
be thirsty again, but whoever drinks the water I give
them will never thirst. Indeed, the water I give them
will become in them a spring of water welling up to
eternal life." The woman said to him, "Sir give me this
water so that I won't get thirsty and have to keep coming here to draw water." He told her, "Go, call your
husband and come back." I have no husband," she replied. Jesus said her, "You are right when you say you
have no husband. "The fact is, you have had five hus-
bands, and the man you now have is NOT YOUR
HUSBAND. What you have just said is quite true."
"Sir," the woman said, "I can see that you are a
prophet. Our ancestors worshiped on this mountain,
but you Jews claim that the place where we must worship is in Jerusalem." "Woman," Jesus replied, "believe
me; a time is coming when you will worship the Father
neither on this mountain nor in Jerusalem. "You Samaritans worship what you do not know; we worship
what we do know, for salvation is from the Jews. "Yet a
time is coming and has now come when the true worshipers will worship the Father in the Spirit and in
truth. "God is spirit, and his worshipers MUST
worship in the Spirit and in truth…" The woman said,
"I know that Messiah (called Christ) is coming.
When he comes, he will explain everything to us."

Then Jesus declared, "I, the one speaking to you—I AM HE." (John 4:4-26)

*Powerful confrontation by Jesus; look what this woman did.

Then, leaving her water jar, the woman went back to the town and said to the people,   Come and see a man who told me everything I ever did. Could this be the Messiah? (John 4:28-29)

*Why is it so important that Jesus spoke with this woman?

*To expand his glory and nature in the earth that all might be saved and display the Kingdom of God in the earth.

Many Samaritans from that town believed in Him because of the woman's testimony, He told me everything I ever did. (John 4:39)

Here's a great quote: *"I remember two things: I am a great sinner and that Christ is the great Savior."~* John Newton (1725-1807), former slave trader and author of the hymn *"Amazing Grace."*

*There's coming a day when you have to follow your conscience, rather than your culture.

Keep trying, keep believing,
and keep hoping.
Never give up!

CHAPTER 11

Around the World

"Don't look for miracles. You yourself are the miracle."
~Henry Miller

God moved mightily in India. During my visit with the people of India, we were out in a remote village, checking out some churches. We prayed for multitudes of beautiful Indian people, who needed healing, and deliverance from oppression. The team and I traveled to one particular village, and some villagers led me to a man. He lived in a hut made of mud and straw. This man did not look well, but those who were inside believed this man would be healed. I walked over to the lame man. "My friend, right now, I come in Jesus' name, I rebuke this sickness, right now, in the Jesus' name. I command this man to be healed." The moment I touched this man, his face glowed; the glory of God was in that little hut. We left this man, believing he received his healing. God touched and revealed himself to many in that village. What an exciting feeling to be in the presence of God.

God is calling each one of his children to share the Good News about the Kingdom of God.

> *And the Good News about the Kingdom will be preached throughout the whole world, so that all the nations will hear it; and then the end will come. (Matthew 24:14 NLT)*

The days are getting darker and darker, and as children of light, we should get brighter and brighter. Don't let anyone or anything draw you away from what God wants to do in your life. We have been quiet for way too long; now is the time to be about the Father's business.

> *And He said to them, "Why did you seek me? Did you not know that I must be about My Father's business?" (Luke 2:49 NKJV)*

We're living in some exciting times from a Christian standpoint. The world has been deceived in thinking there's no need for God; this Antichrist spirit has crept into the schools, courthouses, workplaces, entertainment, and governments and into some churches.

> *The great dragon—the ancient serpent called the devil, or Satan, the one deceiving the whole*

*world—was thrown down to the earth with all his angels.
(Rev. 12:9 NLT)*

God is always talking, but sometimes, we're not listening. Satan is working to divide us. Jesus has taken the keys from Satan and defeated hell and the grave. The world wants to shut us up and throw in the towel, but Jesus says, "I have given you authority over all power of the enemy, and you can walk among snakes and scorpions, and crush them. Nothing will injure you." Let me say this; bad things happen to good people, so realize you may lose your life, but nothing can kill the spirit, which lives forever. I love God's word; we have to read things in their proper context.

> *Don't be afraid of those who want to kill your body; they cannot touch your soul. Fear only God, who can destroy both soul and body in hell. (Matthew 10:28 NLT)*

> *As long as it is day, we must do the works of him who sent me. Night is coming, when no one can work. (John 9:4 NIV)*

We have this wonderful opportunity to teach and preach the gospel of the Kingdom and to heal the sick and raise the dead. Most people who live in this world system are looking for the next drug or drink of alcohol. You can smoke all the weed you want to escape your problems, but you will never get a high like being a child of the Most High God. When you have the King of kings and the Lord of lords, you have the great "I AM".

Let me share with you a powerful visit I had at a local hospital in town. I met a young girl who tried to commit suicide, battling for her life, in a coma. She could not cope with life, so she tried to end her life by taking drugs. I approached the mother and asked if I could pray for her daughter. She gave me permission to pray. I laid my hand on her daughter's head and commanded that her daughter come out of this coma and sin no more. The mother believed God can raise her daughter out of this horrible dilemma; she wanted nothing more than for her daughter to live. I left my phone number and said to the child's mother to call me when she wakes up. God, you're so awesome; my phone rings THREE DAYS LATER. The mother cried out to me with tears of joy over the phone. Her daughter came out of the coma, sitting up in bed eating breakfast on the third day. Halleluiah!

He will be killed, but on the third day he will be raised from the dead. (Matthew 17:23 NLT)

God is still in the healing business, because healing is natural in the Kingdom of heaven. Some people get healed right away, and others go through illness or no healing. God's ways are not our ways; His thoughts are not our thoughts. We must remember God is good, regardless of whatever happens. We are called to believe, to have faith, and the rest is God's business.

> *I tell you, he will see that they get justice, and quickly. However when the Son of Man comes, will he find faith on the earth? (Luke 18:8 NIV)*

I have traveled around the world and met some amazing people, who are hungry for the things of God. The power of God is raising up an army of believers from all over the world, created for such a time as this. God is calling everyone to repentance. I can remember a time in Russia. We were at a meeting, and the power of God hit that church, and many people were healed. Demons were being driven out in Jesus' name, this one lady had a foul spirit, and we commanded that demon to come out, and the next thing you know, she bends over and unleashes this foul vomit. She looked shocked that this foul spirit inhabited her body. She looked at us and thanked Jesus for setting her free. Praise God!

One thing I love about the people in third world countries is they are so hungry for the things of God. They would sit on the ground for hours to hear the Man or Woman of God preach the Good News of the Kingdom of God.

> *But the saints of the most High shall take the kingdom, and possess the kingdom forever, even for ever and ever. (Daniel 7:18 KJV)*

We must be hungry for the things of God; your desire for God must be greater than anyone or anything else. Jesus says, if you love anyone more than Him, you cannot be his disciple.

> *If you love your father or mother more than you love me, you are not worthy of being mine; or if you love your son or daughter more than me, you are not worthy of being mine (Matthew 10:37 NLT). If you put anything or anyone above God, you are in idolatry.*

Your love for God must be greater than your love for your spouse, children, friends, job, business, career, money, and ministry. See what God sees, love what God loves, and hate what God hates. When you love God, you must walk in complete humility, so everyone you meet will experience the love of God. Remember, you have two kingdoms clashing against each other.

Example: The Kingdom of God(KOG) says you should not steal.

Ex: The kingdom of darkness(KOD) says you can take whatever you want. You deserve it!

Ex: The KOG says you should have one wife or one husband to enjoy a lifetime of intimacy with. (Man and Woman)

Ex: The KOD says one woman or one man cannot satisfy their sexual needs.

> *Therefore shall a man leave his father and mother, and shall cleave unto his wife: and they shall be one flesh. (Genesis 2:24 KJV)*

Ex: The KOG says you should love your neighbor.

Ex: The KOD says curse your neighbor.

Jesus went away privately to spend time alone with God the Father.

> *But Jesus often withdrew to the wilderness for prayer. (Luke 5:16 NLT)*

Get away and talk to God and clear all the clutter that's going on in your life. The enemy will bombard you with unnecessary stuff. Stop allowing certain people to monopolize your time with foolishness. The devil loves to distract you and bring all kinds of CAIN (Confusion) in your life.

CHAPTER 12

The Wedding Party

"Problems are not stop signs, they are guidelines."
~Robert H. Schuller

We are living in the last days. Jesus is coming soon. I notice many Christian believers are waiting for the rapture as an excuse not to do the work.

> *And he called his ten servants, and delivered them ten pounds, and said unto them, Occupy till I come. (Luke 19:13)*

We cannot reach the world with the Kingdom of God if we're stuck on saving ourselves only. The day you said yes to JESUS, you acknowledged His death, burial and resurrection. If you want to rule with Him, you must suffer with Him.

Many years ago, I asked my wife to marry me, and she said yes. She's now sanctified (set apart) for me (the groom). The wedding came with a price. It did not matter because I wanted my wife to remember this day for the rest of our lives. Invitations had to be sent out, food had to be prepared, and if you know anything about a wedding, you know you must have a certain number of guests. No more, no less. Each seating arrangement has a wedding plate for each guest; the groom (husband) prepared a place for the bride. Let's see what God has to say about a wedding, the door, and the proper attire. Would you allow anyone to show up to your wedding uninvited? No way!

The bible says:

> He asked him, "How did you get in here without wedding clothes, friend?" The man was speechless. (Matthew 22:12 NIV)

See, this man came in without the right clothes; he came in uninvited through his own self-righteousness. He thought he could do good deeds alone and the wedding host would be happy. Think about the best night club in town; suddenly, some big shot drives up to the front of the club, flaunting their cash. They get out of the limousine, walk up to the bouncer, and wet his palm with a bunch of Benjamin Franklins. I do not care how much money you have; you will not manipulate God with your charisma. Sadly, many people, just like this man, cannot enter the wedding feast, prepared for those who know the Lord.

> *Verily, verily, I say unto you, He that entereth not by the door into the sheepfold, but climbeth up some other way; the same is a thief and a robber. (John 10:1 KJV)*

My wife and I wanted someone who was responsible to watch the door. The only ones to come inside were those who were on the guest list.

> *Jesus says in John 10:9-16 "I AM the door. If any man enter in, he shall be saved, and shall go in and out, and find pasture."*

You must come through the "DOOR" if you want to enter the Kingdom of Heaven. Once we enjoyed the wedding, we were off to the honeymoon, on our way to our new home prepared for my bride. We should be about the Father's business; we'll be operating in the Kingdom for all eternity. I know we've been taught through religious circles to pack our bags and wait for the Lord Jesus Christ to rapture us out of this cesspool of planet earth called SIN.

The bible says (Luke 19:13 NIV) *So he called ten of his servants and gave them ten minas. 'Put this money to work,' he said, 'until I come back.'*

Make sure you're doing God's business to expand His Kingdom everywhere your feet take you before Jesus returns. We must be the light in this dark world. We have two systems in operation, the Kingdom of light and the kingdom of darkness. It's necessary to know God not only saved us, but he wants us to expand His glory to our families, communities, and to the nations. You and I are a vital piece to the plan of God. We must be spotless if we want to enter the Kingdom of Heaven. If you've been to a few weddings, you know pictures are taken before the bride and groom make their way into the hall, where the rest of the guests are waiting. You want to make sure you have no stains/dirt/soil that will bring shame to His name.

When I get to heaven and see all my family and friends, I hope they let me do the "Holy Ghost Electric Slide." Lol!

I love weddings; everything looks so decked out and in order. I can tell you this, according to God's nature; He's a God of order. You cannot bring disorder to a place of order. Heaven is a place of order, and you and I have to be perfect to go to paradise to participate in the Supper of the Lamb. You're probably saying to yourself, "Hey

Dave, what are you talking about being PERFECT?" Yes, I will say it again; if you want to go to Heaven you must be perfect.

> *For I tell you that unless your righteousness surpasses that of the Pharisees and the teachers of the law, you will certainly not enter the kingdom of heaven. (Matthew 5:20 NIV)*

Nobody but JESUS CHRIST is Perfection; He's my "Righteousness," and my "Healer." We must put on Christ's Righteousness as your wedding attire.

> *As it is written, There is none righteous, no, not one. (Romans 3:10 KJV)*

He also became my "Peace." Did he not say He's the Prince of Peace? Jesus said to the religious leaders, I AM is here, standing before you.

> *I AM the way, the Truth, the Life. No one can come to the Father except by me. (John 14:6 NLT)*

You must be perfect to go to the wedding supper of the Lamb. You cannot afford to have on the wrong wedding clothes. We covered earlier in his chapter, you must be perfect, and as humans, we all drop the ball in that department. *Jesus Christ must be your Perfection.*

> *Why do you call me good? Jesus asked. Only God is truly good. (Mark 10:18 NLT)*

We got it now; only God is good. When I was a freshman in H.S., I purchased a knock off gold chain that looked nice, I mean so nice I made sure to give it some extra protection (*coated with clear nail polish*) just in case it turned green.

I want you to say THREE DAYS.

Say it again, THREE DAYS.

On the third day, my gold medallion was dead, and I tried to resurrect my chain with my own efforts (self-righteousness). I had one hot mess on my neck, and the thing turned green.

Say Fake.

Say Fake again.

Just like my own efforts, you cannot outsmart your way into Heaven. Many people will not make it into the Kingdom of Heaven, because they want to do their own thing, just like my fake gold chain. My fake chain FAILED to go through the PROCESS.

Fire will remove any impurities that failed to withstand the pressure. Jesus said, if you want to rule with me, you must suffer with Him. You're not going to get out of this life alive. Don't allow anyone to sell you the idea that life will be a bowl of cherries and you're never going to have any trouble. I love you too much to leave you with this false delusion. God wants to bless you and do some powerful things in your life; however, it will come with opposition. Stay away from the salesman (false prophet) that will tell you everything will always be great and you will have no troubles.

> *I have told you these things, so that in me you may have peace. In this world you will have trouble. But take heart! I have overcome the world. (John 16:33 NIV)*

My necklace was worthless, because it failed the process. Pure 24k gold can endure the process, because it was made to withstand, so we must put our faith in Jesus Christ alone and not in our own good works.

> *All of us have become like one who is unclean, and all our righteous acts are like filthy rags; we all shrivel up like a leaf, and like the wind our sins sweep us away. (Isaiah 64:6 NIV)*

The kingdom of darkness has perverted the institution of marriage. The Kingdom of God defines a marriage between a MAN and a WOMAN.

Marriage is a divine institution, not a human one.

> *So they are no longer two, but one flesh. Therefore what God has joined together, let no one separate. (Matthew 19:6 NKJV)*

Next time you are invited to a wedding, look at all the variables in having a beautiful wedding that will be remembered for a lifetime.

Be relentless like a shark and
devour the word of God
on a daily basis.

Game Plan

"Plans fail for lack of counsel, but with many advisers they succeed." ~Proverbs 15:22 (NIV)

H ere are a few witnessing tips by Evangelist Ray Comfort, one of my mentors, looking at different ways, biblically, to assist you as you share the gospel to those you meet.

> *He leads the humble in doing right, teaching them his way. (Psalm 25:9 NLT)*

<u>Witnessing Tip #1</u>

Start in the natural.

Start with your name and why you are here.

Talk about the weather, sports etc.

Remember the lady at the well. (John 4:1-42) *Please read this incredible story.

Witnessing Tip #2

Swing to the supernatural.

Make an immediate switch from natural to supernatural.

Ask a serious question regarding their eternal destination. (Where will you go if you die?)

Witnessing Tip #3

Open God's law.

Absolute Truth vs. Relative truth.

> *Jesus saith unto him, "I am the way, the truth, and the life: no man cometh unto the Father, but by me." (John 14:6 KJV)*

Witnessing Tip #4

Warn of God's Judgment.

Fines must be paid for breaking the law (Ten Commandments).

Laws and Principles

Witnessing #5

Law to the proud Grace to the Humble

The Law breaks the hard heart

Grace heals the broken heart. (Spiritual part of us where our emotions and desires dwell).

Witnessing Tip #6

Share the Good News.

Very important to know if a proud and self-righteous man will uphold the law.

*If the sinner (law breaker) is broken hearted and contrite, offer Grace.

Let me share with you 18 Principles that will help you as you engage people with the gospel.

Principle #1

A blind (carnal) man cannot see.

Be patient with people and calmly lead them to the doorway to life.

Principle #2

Witnessing and Preaching should involve teaching.

Keep it simple and be respectful as you relate the word to your listener.

Principle #3

Avoid foolish questions.

Be careful you do not go on a Rabbit trail.

Stay focused on the mission.

Principle #4

Aim for repentance, rather than a decision.

We want the Law to break the spirit of pride, so they can be built up in His grace and mercy.

Principle #5

Earn the right to witness.

Be respectful to those with whom you share the gospel.

Principle #6

If God has saved someone, let God tell them.

Let the word of God speak to them. Only God can save, not us.

Principle #7
Never Fear Hecklers.

Audience of One with God.

Principle #8
Be careful of using clichés.

Do you know the Lord?

Backsliders are false converts. (someone who makes sin a life style)

Be sincere in your walk with God.

Principle #9
> For our struggle is not against flesh and blood, but against the rulers, against the authorities, against the powers of this dark world and against the spiritual forces of evil in the heavenly realms. (Ephesians 6:12 NIV)

People are not your enemy; the unseen evil forces are.

Principle #10
Pray for Godly Discernment.

Always pray for those you talk to.

Principle #11

Use the Elements for Amplification.

Speakers, Cameras, smart phone.

Principle #12

Never wear sunglasses while talking to the person you're sharing your faith with. Light to the body is the eye.

Principle #13

Don't let anger with unbelievers upset you.

You are the thermostat, not the thermometer.

Principle #14

Be Honest in your preaching & witnessing (persuade, compel)

Let everyone you minister to feel your passion for the lost.

Principle #15

Read your bible daily.

Loaded with wisdom.

Principle #16

Remember your calling.

Satan comes to destroy. He will try to distract you.

We come to seek and save that which is lost.

Principle #17

Use the word as much as you can.

Become a student of the word, not a religious nutcase.

Principle #18

Use your REAL testimony.

When using these principles, follow the leading of the Holy Spirit. Use wisdom when you engage any disagreements. It's Okay to say I Don't Know if you are tripped up by a question.

> *Certainly not! Indeed, let God be true but every man a liar. As it is written:*
>
> *"That You may be justified in Your words, And may overcome when You are judged." (Romans 3:4 NKJV)*
>
> *So we tell others about Christ, warning everyone and teaching everyone with all the wisdom God has given us. We want to present them to God, perfect in their relationship to Christ. (Colossians 1:28 NLT)*

And then he told them, "Go into all the world and preach the Good News to everyone. (Mark 16:15 NLT)

Yet preaching the Good News is not something I can boast about. I am compelled by God to do it. How terrible for me if I didn't preach the Good News! (1 Corinthians 9:16 NLT)

Biblical evangelism always proclaims the Law to the proud, but grace to the humble.

And he gives grace generously. As the Scriptures say, "God opposes the proud but gives grace to the humble." (James 4:6 NLT)

Thank you all so much for reading my book, prayerfully it will give you the needed tools to win your families and loved ones to Jesus Christ. The methods I and others have used are just tools for you to be well-equipped and empowered by the Holy Spirit. Thank you again and know you are sowing your seed in good ground. I pray you would grab a copy for those you love dearly, who want to share their faith biblically. We believe you will be encouraged by the true stories I've encountered in my walk with Jesus Christ.

Please consider connecting with me as we spark a **FIRE to Evangelize the LOVE of JESUS CHRIST** to

every creature all over the world for the expansion of
HIS KINGDOM.

P.S. If you've enjoyed this book, please consider leaving
a Review on Amazon to help other readers find this information. Thank you!

Connect With Me
Email: dave@igniteyourvisionnow.com
Visit my website:
www.igniteyourvisionnow.com

Prayer of Salvation

If you want to receive Jesus Christ as your Lord and Savior, let me help you by saying this simple yet effective prayer.

Jesus, I made a mess of my life, I'm powerless unless the Holy Spirit empowers me to live a victorious life. I sinned against you by breaking Your holy laws; I repent (change direction/ mindset) from my sinful life and live for You right now. Fill me with Your Spirit, fill me with Your Love, fill me with Your Peace in Jesus name. Amen!

Welcome to the family of God, make sure you read your bible daily, start with the four gospels in the New Testament first: Matthew, Mark, Luke, and John. Make sure you find a good bible believing, bible teaching church that Loves God and Loves people.

> *If we confess our sins, He is faithful and just to forgive us our sins, and to cleanse us from all unrighteousness. (1 John 1:9 KJV)*

Thank you, Jesus, for this new life.

Acknowledgments

I thank God the Father, God the Son, and God the Holy Spirit, the triune God, three persons, "One God." Go therefore and make disciples of all the nations, baptizing them in the name of the Father and the Son and the Holy Spirit.

I thank my two favorite ladies on earth, my lovely wife, Roseline 'Roz', for loving me unconditionally and for her encouragement as I worked on this project for quite some time, and thank you, Mom, Mary B. Bennerman. The love you have for me is priceless. You always believed in me, no matter what. Thank you, Dad, Ernest C Bennerman. Rest in Peace. Love you and miss you dearly. God blessed me with an incredible son, Terrell. Carry on my legacy when I leave this earth. I thank my entire family on both sides. You know who you are. I love each one of you.

Thank you to my brothers and sisters in Christ. I thank my spiritual leaders, Pastor Ronnie Stewart, Pastor Krystal Stewart, Apostle Mark T. Jones, and Lady Lisa Jones, for your covering and prayers. You all are the best; words cannot describe the feeling I have as I express my gratitude for where I came from in my walk as I become more like Jesus and less like me.

Resources

More Books by
Ernest Dave Bennerman

Get Fired UP!

You WHY will make you un-
stoppable. When you understand there will be ups and
downs in life you will have a
victorious mindset; you'll face
life's adversities knowing
they're just part of this journey
to fulfill your Destiny.

GET FIRED
UP!
ABOUT YOUR LIFE
Because If You Don't Who Will?

ERNEST DAVE BENNERMAN

The world needs your gifts. So
allow the words in this book to
encourage, challenge and stir
the gifts that God has planted
inside you.

ISBN 9781522700050

Paperback & Kindle

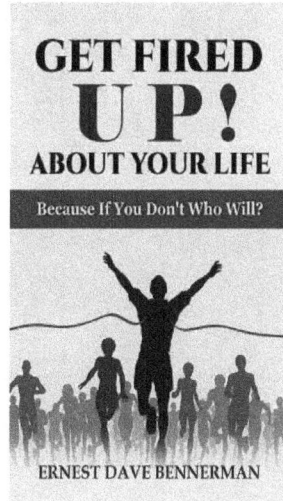

Available at www.IgniteYourVisionNow.com and Amazon

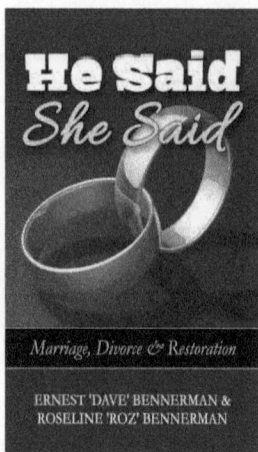

He Said, She Said

Have you ever felt your marriage was in a desolate place, that dry, empty place?

Maybe you're the spouse who feels as though you're pouring everything into your marriage, but it seems as though your spouse has one foot out the door?

In this book, 'He Said, She Said', you'll discover practical and biblical principles to create a lifelong marriage that sizzles.

ISBN 9780997663907

Paperback, Kindle, Audio CD & Audio MP3 Download

Stop the Insanity

If bad credit is holding you back, you can start nursing your ailing credit back to health today with a few strategic moves.

Within this <u>Digital Download</u>, 'Stop the Insanity: Success Strategies for Credit Repair', you'll learn exactly how the credit bureaus' do their business. As well as how to regain their trust step-by-step, and a few simple tricks for being financially responsible

AVAILABLE AS DOWNLOAD ONLY

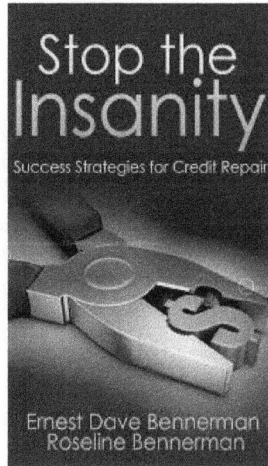

Stop the Insanity

Success Strategies for Credit Repair

Ernest Dave Bennerman
Roseline Bennerman

Available at www.IgniteYourVisionNow.com

Brain Booster

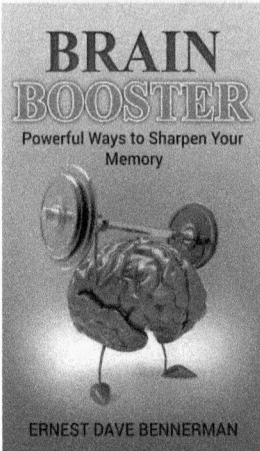

BRAIN
BOOSTER
Powerful Ways to Sharpen Your
Memory

ERNEST DAVE BENNERMAN

If you want to remember names, faces, directions, numbers, occurrences, and nearly every possible information out there, then Brain Booster; Powerful Ways to Sharpen Your Memory will reveal how to transform your brain into a superior power tool that absorbs data like a sponge.

AVAILABLE AS DOWNLOAD ONLY

About the Author

Dave is known as a high octane motivator and speaker on the subjects of Kingdom Building, empowering marriages and confidence building. For the past 20 years, his messages and leadership coaching has helped transform the lives of people through goal setting, life planning skills and accountability measures.

Dave's journey started with humble beginnings. He spent most of his childhood living in the cities of Newark and Irvington New Jersey. Raised by an incredible Mother (Mary) who did the best she could to make sure he and his sister had food on the table and shoes on their feet. Dave, is so grateful for the sacrifice his Mom made.

Dave's biblically-based success and leadership principles have influenced both the church and secular markets. His recent book, 'Get Fired UP! About Your Life Because If You Don't, Who Will?' has transformed the lives of his readers.

Dave is a dedicated lifelong learner. He's a Certified Life Coach and was ordained as an Evangelist at Center for Manifestation in 2012 by the highly-esteemed, Apostle Dr. Mark T. Jones, Sr.

> *"I'm an Evangelist who loves to reach the lost at any cost even if it cost me my life. Love you all and let's make the rest of our lives the best of our lives while we're here on earth and for all eternity." Coach Dave*

Connect With Me

Email: dave@igniteyourvisionnow.com

**Visit my website:
www.igniteyourvisionnow.com**

www.ingramcontent.com/pod-product-compliance
Lightning Source LLC
LaVergne TN
LVHW091219080426
835509LV00009B/1065